My
Selma

Willie Mae Brown

My Selma

True Stories of a Southern Childhood at
the Height of the Civil Rights Movement

FARRAR STRAUS GIROUX
NEW YORK

Farrar Straus Giroux Books for Young Readers
An imprint of Macmillan Publishing Group, LLC
120 Broadway, New York, NY 10271 • mackids.com

Our books may be purchased in bulk for promotional, educational, or business use.
Please contact your local bookseller or the Macmillan Corporate and
Premium Sales Department at (800) 221-7945 ext. 5442 or by email at
MacmillanSpecialMarkets@macmillan.com.
The names of some persons described in this book have been changed.

Library of Congress Control Number: 2022030331

First edition, 2023
Book design by Mallory Grigg and Meg Sayre
Printed in the United States of America by Lakeside Book Company,
Harrisonburg, Virginia

ISBN 978-0-374-39023-5
1 3 5 7 9 10 8 6 4 2

To my mentors, Daisaku and Mrs. Ikeda

To my sons, Boston Snowden and Christopher Brown

To Hundey

Contents

PREFACE

I write these stories of a Selma that I knew and loved. My own Selma. A Selma that brought me joy, troubled me, and baptized me into racial injustice and into the race for justice. I write these stories through the voices of people who lived at the time when I was growing up in Selma. We lived together, schooled together, played together, churched together, and fought together for the same rights as our white brethren who denied us the freedom we were born with. The civil rights freedoms of a people separated by color, ignored by color, despised by color, abused by color, murdered by color. But the color would not fade easily in Selma. That color would not run when it rained. That color did not mix with the white because it stood out when it should have "known its place" in the South.

I write from voices in my memory, I write from being nosy, I write to record the truth about the white people who lived among us, and although in Selma we outnumbered them, they outweighed us because of their color. Let this be known: Not all whites in Selma, Alabama, were hateful. But for many of them, their color was a color of pure, clean hatred.

I write about Selma because our lives have historical precedence in shaping the future. I write so that you may hear, see, smell, and feel the injustice of ignorance but also the sweetness of everyday life, illuminated in my words. In my stories of Selma, much is written in the dialect of the people living there, words I still hear in my head. I thought this was important because it gives flavor to the truth.

Many things played out behind closed doors in Selma and inside my home as the civil rights movement came together outside in the streets. Come with me and look back on a time when men hunted men for game, when the law was always on the side of white.

Wait. Everyone has his or her memories of a place and time when and where they lived. Everyone experiences different things in their towns, their cities, and their states. No two people will have the exact same memories.

Everybody has their Selma. This is my Selma.

I knew what was going on.

My Selma

My Selma

My Selma was a place that emitted the rich, clean odor of black dirt and sour clay, that smelled of sage pork sausages, ham, and biscuits, the breakfast scents all blowing through dew-covered Johnson grass and across foggy highways at five a.m. on any morning.

We sometimes went barefoot outdoors, leaving our shoes up on the porch in case the ground was unbearable. Selma's weather could be hot enough in the summer to blister bare feet on a sizzling sandy sidewalk, or so cold in winter that rag-covered water pipes burst under houses, creating miniature ice castles in the dark.

My Selma was beautiful! With fields of white cotton, corn, long sweet potato vines, and watermelon patches. With untamed land in abundance, thickets where no man had ever walked, and red clay roads where wild game crossed with hunters and dogs in high pursuit.

The sounds of Selma were the late-night lonely whistles of the L&N Railroad trains coming or going, rumbling across the sidings on lower Range Street, not far from our house, and in the mornings, cocks crowing to help raise up the morning sun as citizens prepared themselves for school, work, or church. Radios played the sounds of Wilson Pickett, Tyrone Davis, Johnny Ace, Mahalia Jackson, and Martha Reeves and the Vandellas.

Sunday mornings were dedicated to religious music on those same radios, and to Brown family drives in the country, crowded in the back seat of our Chevrolet station wagon with my three older siblings—Noonchi, Ben, and Louvenia—and my younger sister, Chauncey, in front with Mama and Dah—to Orrville, Alabama, twenty-two miles away from Selma, to attend John the Baptist Church and visit my three mischievous cousins, my quiet uncle Lott, and my wonderful full-body, smelling-good-like-food, pillow-soft-bosomed aunt Susta, who loved to rock Chauncey to sleep on her front porch in her straight-backed rocking chair.

From the car windows I could survey the Selma I knew and loved. Barns with grains in storage and freshly picked cotton for quilt making, sacks of down feathers plucked from pheasants, chickens, and geese, bales of hay in stacks, and root cellars stocked with Ball jars of fruit preserves and freshly canned vegetables put away in the fall as reserve. And, on the sides of the barns, salt licks for the cows in the fields. Beside the barns, our smokehouses were laden with cured hams, beef, and pork shoulders.

Once the fires were lit, our smokehouses were never unattended. At dusk or even in the night, if the menfolk weren't gathered around the fires, sipping drinks, smoking tobacco, joking and gossiping, ghosts and haints of our families past kept watch, still resisting the call from the other side.

Sundays were special in Selma, and everyone knew just about where everyone else was or was supposed to be.

Either you were home or you were in church. On Sundays it was only home or church—even for my older brother!

I know the Selma where Sunday dinners were prepared starting at six in the morning, as the breakfast dishes were being washed. Supper started at half past four in the afternoon with trays of biscuits passed around, dripping with butter and laced with fig preserves cradling the middle.

Visiting preachers and deacons, who were also our teachers at Payne School, Knox Academy, and R. B. Hudson High School, joined us at our tables to speak with us about what was "going on in Selma." The clergy enjoyed Mama's wholesome cooking and tried to show good manners by asking for "just one more biscuit, please," wanting more, yet setting an example at the dinner table for the children, their students.

One of our teachers was the Reverend Frederick

Douglas Reese of Ebenezer Baptist Church, who would baptize me when I was "made ready" at the age of twelve. In 1964 Reverend Reese was president of the Dallas County Voters League, and in 1965, Dr. Martin Luther King Jr. supported his effort to protest against the suppression of Black voting rights by coming to Selma.

Selma's youth were mostly proud and obedient. We attended church on Sundays and respected our elders and our teachers. We never begged and were willing to do work, no matter how menial, to help provide for ourselves and our families. Reverend Reese's sermons on many occasions addressed the youth of Selma as he verbally applauded us for our good behavior.

Selma families kept what little they had as clean and decent as possible. There was always something to give to the have-nots, such as a plate of food or a bag of clothing from a neighbor. If my daddy, Berl Brown, whom we called Dah, knew of anyone hungry, he would drop by with a cardboard box brimming with beans, squash, greens, tomatoes, bread, milk, and meat—Zeigler's souse meat, bologna, or hot links—accepting only a smile as payment.

Dah loved Zeigler's souse meat (also called hog's head cheese). He loved anything that Zeigler's made. He would praise Zeigler's bologna, which could be used as a sandwich meat; it could be warmed and served with a hot plate of collard greens; it could be fried in lard as a break-fast meat, accompanied by grits and eggs. Delicious. And for us children, the red plastic casing around each slice became a toy bracelet or even a ring when twisted around a finger.

The hot links, a bit more expensive, were puffy hot-dog-like sausages that popped in your mouth and spewed savory juices with a little bit of hotness all over your tongue. Zeigler's was king in the South because of their quality meats. Picnics were made perfect with bologna sandwiches, and when church affairs ran low on food, there was always a red roll of Zeigler's bologna and a loaf of pillow-soft Colonial white bread to help fill in the gap.

In my Selma, fruits and vegetables were a part of most meals as well, but not everyone could afford them. Dah had a farm and was generous with what we grew there.

The poor and needy could receive small donations from Selma churches, where used clothing and loose change were offered to tide families over. A good neigh-bor drove the underprivileged to doctors' offices if they were sick. At other times, the disadvantaged would walk, whether they had five dollars for the visit or not. Some-times the families would bring a cured ham, or offer to cut the doctor's lawn or perhaps wash his car as payment, anything to keep their appointments, and the doctor sometimes accepted whatever they offered. However, these bartering exchanges were infrequent because the doctor had bills to pay as well.

There was just not enough to go around for all the people. I saw examples of this every day from a very young age.

I also knew the Selma where Negro preachers, Negro teachers, Negro doctors, Negro florists, and Negro owners of candy stores were revered for having made it. My father made a respectable living working for the railroad, although his job took him away from home for weeks at a time. We of the colored working class drove fine cars: Cadillacs, Pontiacs, and new trucks. Some drove motor scooters, most were willing to assist others when they could. Negro store owners looked out for the youth of Selma and for our families by giving store credit or part-time jobs. Corner stores were convenient places to work and shop because they sold almost anything, including a streak of lean or a piece of fat rib meat for cooking collards or turnip greens.

But also I grew up in a place where Negroes were looked on as less than the people they were, less than human beings, by many of the white citizens.

Listen—and allow me to apologize in advance for the words I am using, but you should know that Negro men, grown men, not just boys, were addressed by whites by their first name or "boy," and Negro women and girls were referred to as "gal" or addressed by their first name, which was arguably less painful than being called a nigger, which was not some misguided term of endearment like some young Black people nowadays bandy about between themselves—"My niggah, what's happnin', niggah?"—No, nah! You were the nigger in the South: shiftless, lazy, dumb, good-for-nothing darkie. And when the term *nigger* was put on you, hostility, anger, and disrespect were attached.

I grew up in a place where white men and white women rode through Negro neighborhoods in posses, on horses, dressed in white sheets with pointed hoods and carrying torches of fire used to set shack houses ablaze and ignite standing crosses on lawns to terrorize Negroes or white "nigger lovers" and set fear in the children.

Dallas County! I grew up in your biggest town, with your people, as a citizen of Alabama, watching white men and white women drive through our town every day with Confederate flags and loaded shotguns on racks in the rear windows of their pickups. AND, dear Dallas County, by the way, I grew up knowing that Negro men had been hunted down and hanged from trees in the backwoods all over your 980 square miles, just like the hundreds murdered all across the Great State of Alabama.

Humph! And let's not forget the Negro citizens who worked as sharecroppers, picking cotton from sunup till sundown for just two, three, four dollars a day.

It was welcome work, it was necessary work, but it was awful hard work.

"You gittin' three, and summa y'all gittin' fo'! We need a bale today and I know summa y'all can brang in a hunnard pounds easy," yelled Old Credo, the Negro straw boss who supervised the twelve to fourteen pickers on the fields Dah rented and cultivated. "Miz 'Gusta been here since five this moaning and it's break time now in a minute, and she already got her hunnard for the day. The way you do it, is you pick with both hands over under, over under. But if you picking with one hand and holding the sack on your shoulder with the other un, you never gon' make any money."

The straw boss yelled, "Miz 'Gusta! You gon' git that rent money by the morrow, right? Mr. Brown gon' give you eleven dollars plus another one fifty on top of dat."

For the landowners and the straw boss, the Negroes' work was never enough.

For the Negroes, the pay was never enough. Never enough to provide food and milk for the young, hungry, sick. Never enough to provide clothing and shoes for the children to attend school. And that's what part of the game was. To hold them niggers down and keep them smiling, keep them in

dilapidated houses,

uneducated,

segregated;

often imprisoned,

or working in roadside chain gangs;

no food,

rotten food,

not enough food.

Suffering every indignation, and castration of body and mind.

In my Selma, a Negro family could be woken up in the middle of the night by a posse of angry drunken white men, pulled from the shotgun shacks they called home, which were then set ablaze because according to the ringleader, "So-and-So up in there owes me money." Babies, toddlers—innocents who were moments ago piled up in feathered beds, cozy with dreams in their heads—now lay wailing in the yard on rock-hard soil, where grass never grows and morning dew clings to nothing, as a wife and mother, clad in a dingy outing gown, scrambles fast to reach a bloodied husband beaten by the white men in their rubber fishing boots—tall white men! Smelling of moonshine and staggering on their feet. Legions of evil, them. All!

Devils gotten loose in Alabama,
Lord,
Ah ah ah men dar rah.

Beatings . . .

lynchings . . .

and other acts of terrorism were the results of anything the raging white man saw fit to kill or destroy as a show of power, sending a message to frighten the people. This ceaseless hostility and pressure put upon the people made it difficult to breathe throughout the South and the Delta.

I grew up in a place and time where white men

looked with lust at Negro women,

made lascivious eye contact with Negro women,

took advantage of Negro women,

under a faraway ebony sky

while silver stars twinkled and all God's creatures hummed live music, witnesses to the crimes of man's inhumanity against woman for the same passion and desire that so condemned many Negro men to death— men tortured and killed with ropes around their necks for disrespecting a white woman by only making eye contact.

Emmett Till! I call your name.

Mack Charles Parker! I call your name.

Willie Edwards Jr.! I call your name.

Willy Webb, Daniel Edwards, Joe Spinner Johnson, I call your names.

Let's not forget Mrs. Viola Liuzzo, killed on a dark Alabama highway by Klansmen and an FBI informant, and so many others destroyed senselessly for their pursuit of justice and equality . . .

I grew up in a place and a town where the right to vote was not allowed to Negroes. Where registration lines stretched several blocks long as people waited, unable to use restrooms, eat at lunch counters, or shade themselves from the sun or rain. Talk "too loud" in line or look at a deputy or sheriff "the wrong way": that was a careless thing to do, especially with the sheriff and his deputies eager to inflict untold suffering and indignation at every chance.

When Negroes finally reached the registration area or the courthouse door, they were told, "We closed!" or poked fun at because some of them couldn't write or spell their names.

"What's wrong wit y'all folks? You cain't spell! You cain't write! Can you sang? Come on, let me hear ya sang sumthin'!"

Then the white registrars would all break out laughing at the humiliation of the person.

Colored folks were always speaking to each other. They didn't have to know you. If they passed you in the street or passed by your house, they greeted you with a "hey" or a wave. But most Negro people humbled themselves in close proximity to whites. Negro men and women quite often stepped aside to allow a white woman to pass as the men tipped their hats and the women cast their eyes low. You had better.

Alabama!

Selma!

I recall the long rows of folks waiting in voter registration lines—of proud, finely dressed colored men in fedora hats and matching coats. Women in elegant dresses, silk sheers or red fox stockings, handbags held on an upright arm or in a gloved hand, with straight-held bodies and serious faces pointed toward the courthouse, a people of pride and integrity, who had awakened that morning with grim determination:

I woke up this morning with my mind stayed on freedom . . . Hallelujah!

I remember hearing first, and then seeing, urine stream from a woman just in front of Mama and me, forced to wait in a nonmoving line for hours, because the reservoir of a tightly held bladder couldn't hold no more! A dam burst and water streamed under her freshly ironed dress and stained the silk stockings as it made its way to a dirt sidewalk.

"Step over that, Hundey," Mama cautioned me, using

my nickname. "Don't step in it, and don't stare at Mrs. Elnora. She can't help it. That's her glory down there."

I stepped over the pool with a wide stride, looking down at the evidence of the struggle for freedom and equality.

Mmm . . .

And I knew the church in Selma called Brown Chapel, where mass meetings were held to educate and instruct the people on the rules of a nonviolent movement. And in order to keep the movement going, the people were asked to contribute what they could and as much as they could.

The people responded. They put in their time to protest, whether rain or shine. Some cooked, some shared their homes; they sang hymns and spirituals, protest songs, prayed in the streets under tents or behind barricades.

One such barricade, a simple rope called the Selma Wall, united a line of green-helmeted police who dared the protesters to cross it. A rope.

The protesters also donated money to the movement, united in the cause for freedom. The right to register and the right to vote. One night I witnessed, in a packed Brown Chapel, coins of the poor, dollars of the poor, raining down from the balcony of the church, from the hands of these struggling people, and landing on the floor of the church, where they were gathered into the offering plates of money. It rained money because the ushers couldn't push through the crowded aisles, couldn't reach upstairs to collect the money, so the people sent it down.

Yes, Selma, then came the clothesline stretched across Sylvan Street, a do-not-cross barrier to prevent citizens from marching on the streets of Selma. Then came the electric cattle prods to keep us in line, just like Sheriff Bull Connor's infamous lawmen in Birmingham, with German shepherds, water hoses, and billy clubs their weapons of choice. Fear tactics! Fear of losing control over the help, the whipping boys, the sharecroppers.

Hear this. Hear this.

Some Negroes in Selma didn't get involved in the movement, nor did they want to have anything to do with Dr. King's nonviolent approach to justice. There were many people in communities of Selma who thought that King was the troublemaker, and these very same Negroes went as far as to chastise their neighbors or family members to "watch out for him, 'cause he ain't doing nuttin' but trying to stir up a mess in here." And over a fence in the backyard, these words: "What y'all going out to those mass meetings for? He needs to go back to 'lanta where he come from and mind his own business." Some frightened Negroes were overheard saying these things.

Dr. King knew this about his people, so he strategized his movement and pushed to wake up the minds of the people by giving them hope, using nonviolent civil disobedience based on his Christian beliefs. Once they awakened, they rose and stood together with him, and came to love him and respect his leadership.

Martin Luther King had become KING!

And in our Selma dialect, *KANG!*

He was the deliverer of a new life for the people of the South. He agitated the government and the haters. He united the youth and the teachers, the old and the progressive, with one mind, a mind to change a low-life condition marked with darkness and despair to one of hope for a brighter future. But a brighter future would take time and patience.

As Martin Luther King Jr. pushed through the South, life continued as it had for years. People carried on their daily activities, shopping, working, mowing lawns, picking cotton, and doctoring the sick. The same people who made it rain money from the balcony of the church, like the housemaids and nursemaids, still rode in the back seats of late-model cars driven by ocean-blue-eyed brides, women with crowns of big shiny yellow hair, teased high and spongy on top of their heads. Or smart-looking innocent brunettes with French rolls who spoke softly in deep Southern tongues, Southern belles, debutantes, or Mrs. So-'n'-So from Summerfield Road.

These white neighbors lived tucked down behind ivy

leaves and moss-hanging trees on the outskirts of town among their kind, with no mind or care of what was going on in Selma.

These women were married to husbands with big money, big stomachs, big ambitions, and big hats who were members of big clubs in big-time Alabama. And these men chased money, chased lust, chased supremacy. They ruled their spouses and wooed other women, both white and Negro, with their small minds and big promises. Their brides were aware of their husbands' lewd and indecent behavior.

Shhh . . . *What's done in the dark comes to light.*

If walls could talk: *Selma! Your secrets are not safe with me.*

Listen! On Sunday, March 7, 1965, six hundred marchers left Brown Chapel AME Church, determined to march all the way to the state capital in Montgomery, fifty-four miles away, to bring their cause to the governor—who wanted them stopped by any means necessary. Just weeks before, in the nearby town of Marion, Negro protesters had been clubbed by policemen, who shot and killed a young man named Jimmie Lee Jackson as he tried to protect his mother. Now, on this day, Bloody Sunday, the lawmen controlled by these same big men stood on the far side of a big bridge in Selma with a dragon's name emblazoned on top—the Edmund Pettus Bridge, built in 1940, named after a "Grand Dragon," as the state leader of the Alabama Ku Klux Klan was known—and used their big wooden sticks and big tear gas masks and big-teeth German shepherd dogs to terrorize a big group of now big-minded emancipated colored people with big determinations to stand UP!

We the people moved forward, and they pushed back, clashing, bashing. They drew our blood. We the people screamed, POLICE! But they were already there, conducting the ambush! They trampled us! They sicced the dogs on us. Smoke, falling, cries, tears, disbelief, citizens, humans, water hoses.

"Oh, it hurt so badly!"

A premeditated attack that threw us to the ground in dirt and onto cement and the Grand Dragon's lettered body lay still above the big open sky, watching, as the terrorists' orchestrated incursion recorded itself into history, proof of the hatred for us, proof of the bigot's mind.

As time will pass, minds put aside the horror as the pain subsides. You now go and build your monuments to this tragedy, like so many more of the proud reminders of lost wars past, with no winners. You, Sinister Sinners of Satan's Selma, one Bloody Sunday in 1965.

I remember it because I was there in Selma. I was not on that bridge that day, nor were any of my family. It happened only weeks after two of my siblings were arrested and imprisoned for a week for getting caught up in another protest, one led by their science and math teacher, Reverend Frederick Douglas Reese. The trauma from that was still with us. And we lived with the conditions that led up to that march—and the repercussions from it—day in and day out, like hundreds and hundreds of our neighbors. I lived Selma every day with my family. My people, Negro people, we were the people of this injustice, the offspring of the King of Agitators, the name given to Dr. Martin Luther King Jr. and the ones who followed him with the unyielding determination to live indivisible with liberty and justice for all, we are those people. Lest we forget. Never forget that We are the People.

A New Neighborhood

There are many things I can't remember about my childhood, but I do remember getting burned by a potbelly stove in the first house in Selma we lived in. I don't recall if I was running around roughhousing or just walking too close to the pitch-black stove, I remember my arm accidentally brushed the belly and got burnt. It wasn't long after that incident that we moved, this time to a larger house, a few long blocks away.

The home that we moved to sat on the corner of Range Street and Second Avenue. We were one of the first Black families to live on the street. Times were changing, and Black people were beginning to move into white neighborhoods. Whites were rapidly moving out.

Dah had a plan to move our family into a bigger house, and the deed of the house that he chose had a second house included. He was worried that he did not have the money to afford both houses and did not want to wait on a loan. Dah admitted to Mama that had he known the house he wanted would become available, he would have set a goal to save money.

Mama listened patiently and said, "Don't worry."

"What?" Dah asked.

"It's okay, Brown. I have the money. The money you've been givin' me for this household. I've been puttin' some of that money away. How much is the house you lookin' at?"

"They want seven thousand dollars," Dah said.

"Oh, they want seven thousand dollars?" Mama replied.

"Yeah," said Dah, "seven thousand dollars."

"Why don't we go to the bank? I have it," Mama said.

"You have seven thousand dollars at the bank? Kate, you fooling me? Where you get that kind of money?" he asked.

"I just told you," said Mama.

Dah was happy. Mama could see the happiness all over his face and she smiled. But Mama could also see his disbelief in her ability to save that amount of money during that time. Dah hugged her so hard he almost squeezed Mama's heart out of her chest. She kept saying, "Stop, Brown. You squeezing my chest too hard."

Now the wonderful day had come. We were moving to a new home.

Dah packed us up along with our furnishings in his pickup truck and moved us out of our small two-bedroom house, which sat close to the railroad station. Our new house was old in age but a fine new house to us. I felt uncomfortable the day we drove the pickup from our old house to the new one. I thought everyone was looking at our old rugs, sparse furnishings, and bags of clothes. When our truck pulled into our driveway on Range Street, my parents' faces glowed. They were proud of our big white house on the corner.

They had worked hard to get the house ready for us to move in. Dah had hired men to clean the chimneys, sand the oak floors, and install a large picture window in front. The men had removed the hearth in the kitchen, a decision that unsettled me because it took away from the beauty and charm of the room.

On the side of the house, there were two large pecan trees. Dah added a clothesline between them.

The difference in our new neighborhood was clearly noticeable. There were proper lawns, and flower gardens in the yards. There were more white people. And not far from our house, there was land that Dah was interested in farming.

Dah had a stable job working on the Southern Railway and had some money saved, and he decided to rent two hundred acres of land from Mrs. Grayson, a very wealthy white woman in Selma. Mrs. Grayson insisted that Dah apply for the lease of the land through her banker, who was happy to do business with Dah based on his reputation with some of the Negro businesspeople in town and his white lawyers, Mr. Howard and Mr. Liston. Dah was approved for the two hundred acres, but it hadn't been easy.

The next morning, I heard Mama and Dah talking in the kitchen over coffee. The white men Dah had gone to see the previous night had all gotten drunk and signed papers to rent him the land he wanted to cultivate.

Dah said, "They didn't want to give it to me at first when I got there, Kate. 'Brown,' they asked, 'what a man like you going to do with all that land? You gon' put a still back there somewhere or build some houses on it?' That's what he asked me. You see how they thank of us, Kate? Like that's all we can do. Let me tell you something, Kate, and I know you read the newspaper every day, so you probably know what the White Citizens' Council is. That council is the first in the state of ALABAMA, right chere in the heart o' their Confederacy, made up of the most important white men in Selma, and it covers the government as well. Their purpose is to maintain how things are handled here. Their purpose is to keep us down. They reject our right to vote, they say how much money we can make doing the same job as a white person, where we can work and where we can't, where we can live and where we can't, all of that. Kate, you see all these delivery trucks out here. Have you ever seen a colored man on one of them?"

She didn't answer. He answered for her. "No you haven't seen one, and nobody else has, because some of them, like Cloverleaf Creamery, have a government contract with the US Air Force and they don't hire Negroes. And that is why the banker and Mrs. Grayson do not have much to say to each other. Mrs. Grayson pulls a lot of strings here for coloreds."

It pained me to hear what Dah had to go through for us, for the sake of the family. To have a prosperous farm, to live in town, to have a rental property, and to be renting and not sharecropping land, Dah was proud. He even made a decision to move his widowed mother from Orrville and into Selma. It seemed like everything was moving upward for us. We were in high cotton, as the saying went.

Given the size of the fields, Dah had to get help from local farmworkers, mostly poor and Black, who needed jobs in Selma. He paid everyone fairly who worked for him, and soon the talk got out that he was a decent person to work for. He had planters and weeders and pickers, and also had someone to dust his fields for insects, like the boll weevils that eat up cotton buds and can destroy a whole field.

At times some of the workers didn't show up, and because they had no telephones to call in, Dah could find himself stuck without help. When this happened, he relied on us children to help. We also had to pitch in if heavy rains were predicted. Alabama is known for tropical storms and flash floods. Heavy rains can ruin a cotton field that is ready for harvest, and that's when we had to go into the fields to help before the rains came. Sometimes we could miss up to a week of school just getting the cotton out of the fields.

Picking cotton by hand under the harsh Selma sun was broiling-hot, backbreaking work. The big fluffs of white cotton had to be picked free from the prickly bolls all up and down the waist-high stalks and put into long bags that we pulled behind us on a shoulder strap. Each bag might hold fifty pounds of cotton and would take hours to fill. No one was happy about this work, and we cried all the way on the drive to the field. We felt it to be the most degrading, painful thing to do, and we didn't get paid. Dah was angry with us when we did not want to help. Mama couldn't say anything to Dah because he would lash out at her.

As a young child, I suffered with nosebleeds, but

they never seemed to come when I wanted to get out of working in the fields, and always showed up when I wanted to play baseball in a nearby empty lot with my friends. Never did I have a nosebleed in Dah's field. I couldn't even pick my nose enough to make it bleed in the hot sun.

When the work was behind us and the cotton was finally out of the field, everyone was happy as we drove the harvest over to Butler's Gin on the old truck that had once brought our belongings to the new house. That old truck was army green, with wooden rails built up high to hold cotton. There were two cotton gins in Selma— one belonged to Dick Hauser, and the other belonged to Jim Butler, a Negro man. Cotton gins were big, dirty, noisy machines that seeded and combed the raw cotton, which was then put into bales weighing up to five hundred pounds.

The Hausers could be difficult, but they had also known my grandfather, Andrew, and there was an understanding between Grandfather and the Hausers ... a mutual respect. Whenever Dah was in Orrville, he purchased his products from Mr. Hauser's grocery store. Hauser's grocery had the best hook cheese in the state of Alabama. Most southerners called cheddar cheese with a black wax casing hook cheese because it hung from a wrought iron hook in the general store.

But still Dah preferred to bring his cotton to Jim Butler.

When we drove our load that made the two bales of cotton one year, the truck was leaning to the side, and Dah was driving with his long arm out of the window, holding a Winston cigarette. He was proud, driving the truck with me in the middle and my older brother Ben, who we called Maine, next to me in the cab by the window. I was uncomfortable for two reasons—the coarse horsehair padding coming up out of the torn leather seat cushion was one thing, and not wanting to be seen working was the other. Dah was smiling, and I learned to smile, too, once I saw how much he was paid for the cotton. I also smiled when the vegetable harvest came in, and I smiled when we had everything for the winter and school and a new tractor and a bank book with a two in front of four zeros that I should not have seen. I cried when I got caught being nosy.

Dah's mother had ten children, and they all helped in different ways to move her into Selma. Grandmama moved to First Avenue and Church Street, where a few other older ladies lived on the same street. They were all friendly and tended gardens, loved God, and had children whom they bragged about. Most of them were widows. My grandfather was also deceased, which didn't stop Grandmama from bragging about him and her children who held down government jobs or were married to working men or living up north. One daughter was a nurse, another a teacher. Our grandfather had been a successful barber in Orrville, and a successful farmer. "Not a sharecropper like my daughter," Grandmama would say of my aunt Susta, "though she is an excellent cook, clean, God-fearing, good with money, and loves her family."

Grandmama's back porch was a screened-in sitting room decorated with rattan chairs and ferns. There was a bathroom with a sink and tub, with separate little toilet and shower rooms, and a smaller bedroom, where I would stay when she needed company overnight. This bed and mattress were both handmade. The bed frame was made of iron, and the box spring was iron coils forged together and sat on plank slats. On top of this was a mattress covered with striped, heavy cotton ticking, with thick strings of heavy thread intertwined throughout the mat to reinforce the field cotton and a layer of horsehair underneath. Next came Grandma's feather bed, also covered by the thick ticking so that we were not pricked by the feathers. Her handmade quilts held me in place once I was under the covers, but didn't prevent me from sinking low into the bed and sandwiching myself into the feathers. Once I had dropped down in the bed and was wedged in low, I fell asleep to the sound of the mantel clock in her bedroom and the crackling of her fire.

A very spiritual woman, Grandmama prayed a lot.

Dah showed her a lot of respect, and so did my mother. Grandmama was special to us children. If we knew that she was walking over to our house for a visit, there was always a stir to get everything clean and neat before she put a foot on the front porch. We had to be on our best manners and greet her when she was in the house.

We knew Grandmama better than our mother's mama, who lived far away in Choctaw County, over by the Mississippi border. I remember when she came to visit us once in our new home for two weeks in the summer. Her name was Lela, a dark, short, attractive, and funny woman with a strong chiseled nose.

Dah had met Mama in a café one day in Bessemer, Alabama, where she was attending school and working part-time in the café. For his job laying track for the railroad, Dah often traveled to other towns. He was allowed to drive machinery. This was a privilege because most Negroes were not trusted to use trucks and other equipment. He met my mother again on one of those trips passing through the same town, and by now he was smitten with her and soon they started their courtship. My mother was living at the time with my great-aunt and had to consult her as to whether or not she could marry my father, who was constantly asking her to wed him. Finally, they got in touch with my mother's mother and she gave them her blessing. After their marriage, they moved to

Orrville and lived with my father's mother, who taught Mama many things about life and the church.

The church was where my mother learned to play piano by ear. Once she was married, she took to learning embroidery and quilt making. She stopped playing the piano. As an adult, finding these things out, I became upset that we were never taught piano or encouraged to play. I held it against her for some time.

I did have the pleasure of making a quilt with my mother once and learning some things about stitching. Dah, pleased with my sewing, would often ask me to darn his pants. I became better at the craft knowing he would appreciate it.

Next door to our rental home was a narrow alleyway, and after the alley was a two-story white building consisting of a small repair shop, which had lettering on the bottom of the street-side window: FRED'S RADIO REPAIR. Mama said Mr. Fred sometimes had problems paying his bills, and there were sometimes notices from creditors pinned to his door, threatening to shut him down for nonpayment. During those times his place was frequently dark.

A narrow set of stairs sat inside the middle of the building, giving way to a leased apartment upstairs, where

Mrs. Callie Mae Robinson resided. Mrs. Callie lived alone and didn't go out much. It was rumored that she liked Mr. Fred and that they were together as a couple. She mostly kept to herself unless she spied a friendly neighbor. Her conversations with those she liked took place from her top-floor window overlooking the street, while whomever she spoke to stood below on the sidewalk. If you looked up toward her window in passing, you would often see her sitting there, elegantly dressed up with powder and red rouge on her lips and cheeks. Mrs. Callie had a view of everything going on.

I may have been one of the only people on the block to ever go into her home. One time Mama had me go up the stairs and get a piece of ginger molasses bread from Mrs. Callie and bring it back to her. Mama had just spoken to her from the sidewalk, and Mrs. Callie had offered her a taste and wanted Mama to let her know if it was good.

"Now, get a good look at the house while you're up there," Mama instructed, "and thank her for the cake before you leave."

I discovered that the mysterious Mrs. Callie kept a clean home with lots of accents on the color red, lots of knickknacks and souvenirs, little glass poodles on the coffee table and decorated plates on the walls fenced in with wire holders. There were crocheted cotton scarves on the backs of chairs and arms of the sofa. A large scarf fashioned as a round dish held a white bowl of silk flowers in its pink-and-white design. The footstool in front of her sofa was upholstered in a red tapestry of Chinese fans, matching the red wool rugs on her floor and the lipstick rouge on her face. Everything smelled like perfume. I took the cake wrapped in wax paper and delivered it to Mama.

On the next corner lived Mrs. Rutgers and her family. They owned the gas station across the street on Range and a few other buildings on First Avenue. The Rutgers were a big, loving family and their house had once been connected to an old feed-and-grain store. Block-painted letters reading FEED & GR were just visible on the faded red front of their building. The rest of the old sign was gone. We Brown family children grew up with Mrs. Rutgers's colorful offspring as our playmates. Music was always pouring out of their house, and it was a popular gathering place for neighborhood men, women, and curious children. On any Friday or Saturday evening, there might be a card game underway, or a fish fry.

Our neighbors directly across the street from our new place were white. The Randalls were beekeepers. Mrs. Randall, a sweet, round-faced lady with a pleasant voice, brought over a jar of honey one day as a welcoming gift and introduced her son, a tall, lanky teenager. Mr. Randall did not come over. I had never met this white man before, but I studied Mr. Randall carefully from afar. I enjoyed sitting on our front porch watching him tend the hives as he moved in slow motion, covered in gloves, a white suit, and a big hat with netting. He almost looked like an astronaut, and even the smoker he carried in his gloved hand to calm the bees when he opened the hives looked like an exotic bit of outer-space equipment.

When he wasn't hidden inside his beekeeping uniform, he always seemed to be neatly dressed in the same white shirt and gray slacks, even when he was doing yard work. He drove a blue Ford Falcon with a white interior. I watched him wash that car many times. His long driveway off Range curved 'round to the back of his property. The yard was filled with lots of trees and boxwood shrubs.

We hadn't been in our house long before he started a conversation one evening with Dah on the sidewalk out front. I was watching through the screen door and could hear them speaking in what sounded like a friendly manner. But what was being said didn't sound so friendly.

It seemed like Mr. Randall could not accept the newcomers that were moving into his neighborhood.

"Lots of turnover happening around here, Brown. Lots of changes. I can't say I'm happy about them."

I couldn't hear Dah's mumbled reply.

"Now, understand, I've got no problem with you,

Brown, as a man, or with your family. You seem like decent folk. But I don't want the neighborhood to be saturated with different folks."

Now Dah's reply got louder and I could hear his words clearly.

"You don't want to have a problem with me, Mr. Randall. And it could only happen that you would have a problem if you get out of your place. With my work, I'm not home often, and I expect things to be the same way coming home as when I left home. I don't want any trouble."

Our neighbor seemed taken aback by this and ended the conversation as quickly as he could, hurrying back across the street.

From that time on Mrs. Randall brought more and more little gifts from their hives over to the house. "More hundey for my sweet Hundey," Mama said as she handed me the latest jar to put up in the pantry. My siblings all thought it was hilarious. Often we had so much honey and honeycomb in the house, Mama had me take the new jar straight out the back door and hand it over to Mrs. Elnora, who lived in the back of us, and when she had more than three or four jars, she'd share hers with the Swains, who lived next door to her.

All the honey in the world couldn't sweeten Dah's opinion of his neighbor. And the neighborhood kept on changing in ways that didn't suit Mr. Randall and other whites like him, and soon the Randall family would move away to Florida, not long after President Kennedy was assassinated in 1963, when I was ten years old.

The day in November that President Kennedy was shot, my classmates at Clark Elementary and I cried at our desks when we heard, and Wayne Smith hollered out in the classroom, "We are all going to die because we don't have a president!"

The shooting happened right around lunchtime. Mrs. Jones, our teacher, was called to the office and returned to the class to tell us the news and dismiss us. We were told to walk home together if we lived near each other. I walked with Wayne to his house and then continued on home. When I got home, our television was on and the newscaster was saying the president had died. His vice president, Lyndon Johnson, would be sworn in as our new president. We all cried for President Kennedy and for his family.

For days, our television remained turned on, seemingly waiting for something to happen, and before long it did.

"They got him, they shot him!" Noonchi shouted out the back door.

"Who shot who?" Lou hollered.

"Jack Ruby just shot the president's killer, Lee Harvey Oswald. He blasted him right on TV, right in his gut!"

We ran into the house and there it was. Everything my sister had said was true. Two days after assassinating the president, the killer was dead.

It took us all about a month to overcome the tragedy of losing the president. It seemed like whites and Negroes were equally sad. Flags flew low at banks, schools, and churches, as people everywhere mourned with Jackie Kennedy and her children and so did we, right there on the polished hardwood floors of our new living room.

First Week of Summer

I found the phone book on the coffee table in the living room. It was not in its proper place, which would have been resting underneath the telephone on the little table in the corner of the room. Lots of things in our house were always finding new places for themselves because some of us were lazy, and putting things back where we had found them was hard to do.

Mama's coffee table was supposed to hold the ashtray, which was never used, and a few issues of *Jet* and *Ebony* magazines, stacked up neatly next to a bowl of hard candy. Sometimes things like a dirty plate, a set of jacks, a jump rope, a board game, or rickrack and a spool of thread and needle found their way haphazardly on top of the table. When it got too disorderly, Mama ordered Noonchi, Lou, or me to get a rag and dust off the table and "put some of that junk away."

Usually it was me who got the job. And when it was

complete—and I mean complete, because I couldn't just dust the table and leave it at that, I cleaned everything in the room and then even mopped the hardwood floor—Mama would pass through the doors and remark, "Now, don't that look better, Hundey?" as if I was the one who had messed things up in the first place.

This morning I had made up my mind that now that I was almost a teenager, I was going to find a real job that paid me to work, and I was going to use the phone to call as many people as I could to get hired. I told Mama first thing. "That's nice, Hundey," she said as I helped her with the dishes. That made me happy, but I also knew I hadn't told Mama everything I was thinking about this job search.

The first thing I did was make a list of the Negro women I knew who were mothers and might need to do some errands without their children. Then I asked for my sister Noonchi's help to make a list of all the white people who might need a babysitter for the summer. I had never done any babysitting outside my neighborhood before. This summer Noonchi was a full-time volunteer candy striper at the Anderson Nursing Home, and she had lots of experience babysitting.

Then I had to set different prices for each group: Negro women, two dollars an hour, and white women, three dollars an hour. Mothers in my neighborhood always thought my price was too much to pay, yet they ended up paying what I asked for because they knew I did a good job. Afternoons, I helped the children with their schoolwork. Evenings, I could be relied on to bathe their little ones and wash their hair and plait it before the parents got home.

I felt responsible enough, having watched my younger sister Chauncey for Mama ever since she was in diapers, and though I hadn't talked about trying to go work for a white mother, Mama always said that we needed to stop asking her for money and get a job.

After finding the phone numbers for all the names on my list, I ran a glass of water from the sink and started practicing what I would say when they answered the telephone: "Hello, my name is Willie Mae Brown, and I am Kate Brown's daughter here on Range Street in Selma. I am looking for a job with children for the summer. Would you have one or know of one?"

I thought that sounded good, so I practiced it for a while and tried adding a smile, because Mama said people could feel smiles on words over the telephone.

Then I made my first call, dialing the numbers carefully around the circular dial on the phone.

On the first two calls, I reached a busy signal. The next was the receiver of a phone being slammed down in my right ear. And the next one answered the call but didn't need any help.

After that, I gave up and sat outside on the front porch in the swing. School had been out for a few days now, and I had nothing to do but sit in a swing or go to the country to visit my aunt Susta and her children, who were nice cousins most of the time. But when Frankie and Cookie were bad, they were really bad.

When the devilish functions were in them, my cousins might knock me down during a game of chase and then pin me to the ground and torture me by letting snot run out of their noses and then sucking it back up. Or they would try to make me eat mud pies, for real. The worst was waking me up from a deep sleep by shoving a screaming kitten in my face.

Picturing all this got me thinking I better make some more phone calls.

The next few were not good. Another person slammed down the phone, one couldn't hear what I was saying, and then a man answered the next call and breathed heavily in my ear.

I was about ready to give up but made one last call to a woman named Mrs. Nichols, a white woman who Noonchi had done some work for. She had two children, a boy and a girl. Mrs. Nichols was divorced and lived out going toward Craig Air Force Base, in a trailer court with her children, working as a bartender. Our conversation was short, but I felt hopeful. She said she did need some help and would be in touch with my mother to hear what she said about me working for her. This seemed promising! I felt a tremendous amount of joy about possibly having a summer job.

Mama spoke to Mrs. Nichols the next day after she called our house. Mama told her, "I'll speak to my husband and get his opinion on this." When she hung up, she gave me a look.

"What's the matter, Mama?" I asked.

"You should have told me you were looking to work for a white family this summer," she said. "I need to think on this, and you know your dah will have something to say."

Dah came home off the roads a few days later, exhausted. He had been in Kentucky, laying crossties and track for the Southern Railway. It was a job he had worked on since he was fifteen years old. His job took him away two to three weeks at a time, and when he returned home for two to three weeks, he worked the land he had leased from Mrs. Grayson. Dah was strong and serious about his work. He was an honest man to his family and his responsibilities. When he was not out working the fields with Ben, weeding the vegetables, picking beans off the vines, or checking for fire-ant nests, he was socializing with Mama. They enjoyed sitting out on the porch together, talking sometimes till late, sometimes just saying little or nothing at all. Once a month he went to Beloit, Alabama, to the Masonic Lodge for a meeting.

The first thing Dah always did when he came home was get cleaned up. Then he and Mama liked to have some private time together.

I was nervous about Mama asking Dah about me getting a job, and I could imagine just what he'd say: "Kate, you must be out of your mind! What is wrong with you? There's plenty of work around here that them chillren can do 'stead of going out there taking care of that woman's chillren. If Hundey wants something to do, let her get some of my khaki pants and work shirts darned for me and put them in the machine and wash them. There's a whole lot of freezer bags in there waiting on someone to shell those paper-shell pecans that's falling off them trees. Let her do that."

While I was out in the living room playing with Chauncey, I listened to the murmur of their conversation, imagining my chance to work for Mrs. Nichols slipping away. My heart pounded when Dah called out to me. "Wil' Mae," he hollered. "Come here! Now!"

"Yes, sir, I'm coming," I said loudly.

I raced down the hallway and nearly tripped over the threshold, just missing Mama.

Mama didn't say a word. She just stood in the doorway of his bedroom with one foot out of a pair of slides, propped up on the calf of the other leg, her soot-black hair full and heavy, hanging in her face. The strap of her slip lay off her shoulder, black against her clay-colored baked skin.

Dah was sitting on the side of his bed with a roll of money in his hand the size of a newborn's fist. He handed it to Mama. She reached for it and the black strap tightened.

"Put that there away. We talk 'bout it tonight." Then he turned to me. "Listen. What you doing right now?" he asked me.

"Nothing," I responded.

"Okay, you not doing nothing?"

"No, sir," I answered.

"You know where Maine at?"

"Yes, sir, he went to East Selma," I said.

Dah looked at Mama as if to say, *I told you so.* She kept quiet, knowing Brown felt that Mildred's daughter Evelyn had too much of a hold on his son.

Mildred White was one of the women who opened

their homes to feed and host the dignitaries coming into Selma. I was told by her daughter that one night several Negro men came by Mildred's house in East Selma as usual and this time Dr. King was with them. They told Mildred that they were trying to get Dr. King out of Selma, but they were having some difficulties, knowing that the police would be watching them. They said that King's life was in jeopardy and if she could do this favor for them, she would have to understand that it would be a life-and-death situation. She was asked to drive Dr. King to the airport in Montgomery. They would meet her there and escort him onto the plane. She agreed and smuggled Dr. King in her car under a pile of quilts, taking the back roads to Montgomery. Driving at the legal speed to the airport, she was never stopped by police officers. There she met the men at the airport, and she turned Dr. King over to them and returned home safely.

Mama often said that she knew Brown was afraid Maine might make a mistake and that gal come up pregnant before Maine finished school. She also knew Dah had had a drank. He always did after leaving the gang to come home. It was relaxing for him, and she knew how hard it was for him to face those nasty men he worked with every day for the few weeks he labored among them. These were men he despised, but he had to endure and keep working. He had to keep a smile as often as he could remember to show one, and to address them as *mister* or *boss*, or say *yessir* when he meant *no, sir*.

Dah always said the white men he worked with were the worst. "Them crackers always trying to start a fight, calling me bad names like coon, nigger, darky, crow," he'd say. They had a knack of spitting their chewing tobacco close to his shoes and grinning about it. Dah said once, "They like to pick at people. And if you say anything to one of them, all of them who are close to the instigator will team up on you, and then the boss will blame the victim." Dah said he learned to pay them no mind, which burned him up inside.

"I'm worried about that boy of ours, Kate," he said.

"I know you are," Mama said. "But she's a nice girl, Brown. Her mama's a good lady. An important lady."

"That's not what I mean. I'm worried about him out there among all the white men. They some low-down suffering son of a guns out there, Kate. Wild and untamed. They can do some thangs reg'lar white men don't do, but the reg'lar white man nowadays can't be trusted, either. You have to study them all. Keep an eye on 'em. Just don't let them know you watching 'em. First thang they want to do is pull that pistol off they hip. They rough now, and if you go up 'gainst one, you might as well kill him and run, 'cause they got the law on they side no matter how po' they is. And don't think just 'cause he laughs with you or smoke tabakkur with you he your friend. Nah, that piece of trash will tell you straight out, I'm gonna blow yo' brains out. You'd better believe him. That's why, and I say this in all honesty, 'cause it can be thirty years from now but that cracker will still be the same. Hell, he may clean hisself up, come out to be the richest man in town, but he da same: low-down!"

Dah lit a cigarette and blew the smoke out hard, as he continued to speak. "I don't trust them one bit, Kate. We living in some hard times, and you have to be hard to live in these hard times. I just come 'cross the Pettus Bridge a while ago and couldn't git 'cross Sylvan Street. People everywhere. They got all that blocked off." He waved his hand as if to shoo away something. "Thangs hard here, and everywhere you go, somebody's child missing. Ain't been home in a while and, you know sumpthing, that child ain't coming back. It's hard out here and that's how I'm raising my son in these hard times, and if times change, I'm gon' raise him differently, but that ain't gonna be too soon, so just bear with me for a while, honey. Thangs gon' get better, but I got to do what I got to do for my family."

"Brown, I got something to say about all this now, but

first, what you mean by 'hard'? I don't want my son getting in any trouble out there. Explain yourself," Mama demanded.

Dah cleared his throat. "What I mean is that I want him to have the 'sight to know when he may be in danger or y'all in danger and take the courage to do something about it. I don't mean for him to go out there and just start something with someone 'cause he can. He must be able to think correctly, Kate, and know when he right. Sometimes he may have to run, sometimes he may have to take a stand. I have taught him as much as I know. All of them been taught and they also learn from books in school. Now what the white man's talking is different, can't be learned in school. Ben needs to know how white men think, and I b'lieve he understands. And on top of that, he got to watch his own kind. Some Negroes git to drinking and lying, and you got a mess on yo' hands."

Dah went quiet and finished smoking his cigarette. Then he seemed to remember what he wanted me to do.

"We gon' to the fields after I have my bath, your mama, me, Maine, and anyone else who wants to go. One of you chillren needs to stay here to keep an eye on things, I don't know which one. I want to check on things out there. Wil' Mae, call over to Mildred White's and ask to speak to Maine. When he gets on the phone, tell him I want him to come meet me in the field or back here, whichever, dudn't matter, and hang up! Don't get into no commersation with him, 'cause I know him and he gon' want to know what I'm feeling so he can gauge how many mo' minutes he can spend with that gal of Mildred's."

I made the call just as Dah had instructed. When I went back to his room to tell him the call had been made, the bedroom door was shut, so I knocked. Mama instructed me through the door to put on some long pants and a shirt and wait for them on the front porch.

"But first," she said, "go look on my dresser and get a quarter for yourself for a cold soda at Deak D'Ampars's store. And don't slam that screen door. And, Hundey, before you go, run some water in the bathtub for your father, please."

It wasn't long after I'd done all this that Maine was pulling up in the yard. The Oldsmobile turned slowly into the driveway. Through the open windows I could hear an unmistakable voice singing all about swinging Papa and his brand-new bag.

We owned two cars, the Chevrolet station wagon and an Oldsmobile sedan, and Ben drove the Oldsmobile most of the time. The station wagon was used for going to the grocery store and church, or when Dah was home. Maine didn't get out of the car until disc jockey Ace Anderson called James Brown's name.

"Hey, Hundey, has Dah been calling for me?" Ben asked. And before I could answer, he asked, "Where you going?"

"I am going to Deak's to get a Coke-Cola and some oatmeal cookies. You better go see what he wants before he comes looking for you."

"Mama in the house?"

"Yep."

"She in her room or back there wit' him?"

"She with Dah," I said, walking away.

"Willie Mae," Ben called to me, running down the sidewalk. "Is he all right today or is he mad about something?"

"No, he ain't mad about nothing. Neither is Mama. They going out to the field to check the crop and want you to come."

"Which field he talking about going to?"

"I don't know. Just go see what he wants. I'll be right back."

"Okay. Well, here, take this and bring me a Pepsi back," he said, running his hand deep into his pocket.

"Wow, five dollars! So can I get something out of here?" I asked.

"Yeah, go ahead and get what you want," he said. "Bring me back my change, though."

"Thanks, and by the way, you better tuck your shirt in fo' Dah sees it. You know how he is 'bout that."

Dah adored Ben and they were the best of friends. When Dah was on the road, Mama looked to Maine for support in taking care of our land and the fields. He was also responsible for being the man of the house. Dah had taught him everything: how to drive machinery, cars, trucks—automatic and manual. Dah taught him how to plow, hoe, fight, shoot guns. He instructed him on traveling the back roads of Alabama, and how to talk to white folks, especially the sheriff and his deputies in Dallas County. At sixteen, Ben knew how to pump gas and change a tire on any of the machinery, and he knew how to negotiate, whose hand to shake in a deal, and how to bank, when to speak, when to run, walk, court girls, and anything Dah himself knew, including hygiene and dressing well. Even in the fields, Dah and Ben wore work clothes—bright white T-shirts, clean khakis or blue jeans.

Mama said that from the day Ben was born, Brown was a changed man. He finally had a son. Shortly after Mama gave birth to Ben, Dah jumped in his truck and drove around the neighborhood, blowing his horn and telling everyone he met that he had a son. When things finally calmed down after a few days, Mama said that Dah asked her if he could take care of Ben exclusively. "Kate, you take care of our firstborn, our girl Noonchi, and I'll take care of Ben, meaning I'll teach him everything he needs to know about being a man. And you teach Noonchi the things girls should know and do. But, Kate, I want you to still be their mama as far as it comes to taking care of them and feeding them and washing them, you know what I mean. I just want to make sure that Maine is well set in this house in case anything happens." He took Ben mostly everywhere he went in his truck and started teaching him to drive at eight years old.

I loved Ben, too. I think the first time we became close was when I was about eight years old and contracted the measles. It started on my stomach and Mama caught me scratching a lot, lifted my shirt, and found the bumps. Within days, I was covered from head to foot, and so were Noonchi and Lou. We couldn't scratch because Ben kept warning us not to. My grandmother sent corn shuck to make tea for me to drink and wash in.

The measles had broken out just as the high water came and flooded Selma. The low-lying areas were flooded so badly that caskets from the cemetery in East Selma floated on top of the water, and the stench of freshly buried bodies was evident. Dah was away working and Mama was busy looking after Chauncey. Noonchi, Lou, and I were all afraid to go to sleep that night, thinking that we would wake up and have a skeleton in our yard. Ben assured us that our thinking was false. He spent more time in our bedroom than he did in his, sleeping in the chair until early morning. We all slept better because of him. The floods of 1961 didn't reach our home but did reach a lot of homes in the downtown Selma area.

Deak's store smelled of things delicious and wholesome to eat when the door was opened. I stepped into the smell of licorice and sugar cookies, ham and sawdust. There was also the heavy scent of brown paper bags, oak floors, newspapers, oil paper, onions and dill pickles, grains, meal, flour, and spices. Oh! How I loved going into that place, where Mrs. Mass, a tall gray-haired woman with good manners, was the store clerk. She was so very kind, and to children especially. If you were a child and you had a penny and oatmeal cookies were two cents, you left with an oatmeal cookie or a sucker, or ice cream or push-ups, which were a nickel, and sour balls, twelve for a dime.

Mrs. Mass worked in an apron tied around her waist, and she was behind the counter every day 'cept Sunday. On Saturdays she left the store at three p.m. to do her sewing. She made the aprons herself, and starched and ironed them weekly. After work each day she'd fold the apron she had worn and put it in her pocketbook and walk past our house to go home. She didn't have a husband. She had God, and she had a son named Cero.

Cero Mass was a talented and creative tailor who worked from home, making men's and women's clothing to order. His popularity for turning the heads of the ladies in Selma's Negro community was well known, not only for his handsome appearance but also his soulful singing, which brought the Ebenezer Baptist congregation to their knees praising God.

On Sunday mornings Cero sang deep within his throat as the pastor was receiving the flock, and the gathering congregation felt the spirit, shouting and fainting, as the ushers descended on the rows to fan ladies overcome by the Holy Ghost. While he sang, Reverend Reese called out in a melodic voice, "Come. Just as you are. The church doors are open. Come and sin no more."

Today Mrs. Mass met me at the counter with her clean gray hair pulled back in a bun. "How are you, baby? How's Mrs. Brown doing? She all right?" she asked.

"Yes, ma'am, she fine."

"Everybody okay?"

"Yes, ma'am. We are getting ready to go to the field in a minute," I said.

"Do me a favor?" Mrs. Mass asked as she put my items in the paper bag. "Ast your mother to save me some cantaloupes when she get some more, about three be fine. I want to take them out to Anderson Nursing Home for Mrs. Rita. Po' thang. Nobody helping her much since her son passed. I thank them cantaloupes be good to brighten her up." She didn't use the cash register to ring up my items. She did it in her head and then checked her totals with a pencil on a brown paper bag. "Give me two dollars and sixty cents, sugar," she said, as I passed the money to her. "You sho' Katie want you to have all this chere candy and stuff you got up here in this bag?"

I smiled. "I will tell Mama, Miss Mass. And Ben did give me some money for a Pepsi-Cola, so I am gonna spend a little mo' for me." I laughed.

"Whoo, you gon' make that boy mad now. Then Katie gon' hafta separate y'all."

"No, she won't have to do that, Miss Mass. I am always doing some things for him. I help him wash his car, polish his shoes, and I hang up all his clothes when he pulls them out his closet and be too lazy to put them back," I said.

"You do? You do all that for him?" she asked in a lady sweet voice.

"Yes, ma'am, I do it," I said. And then for some reason I blurted out, "But this summer Ben is going to have to take care of himself. I just got a babysitting job with a white woman across town."

"Well, my goodness. That's a big job, but I think you're up to it. Yo' mama always told me you were a good girl, and I want you to stay that way. You hare me?" she said, pointing her finger at me. "That way if you good," she went on, "God's gonna make a place for you in heben. Okay, now go on back home and tell Katie what I told you."

"Yes, ma'am," I said, waving to her as I rolled the top of the bag down to a handle.

Dah was putting a hoe in the back of the car when I walked into the yard, and Mama was in the front seat looking magazine-pretty and glowing. She had run a hot comb through her hair to straighten it out some. We could see she was happy and so were we. Dah was home.

I jumped into the back seat, where Noonchi sat with Chauncey, and waved bye to my sister Lou standing in the yard. "Mama, when did Lou get home from the choir rehearsal, and do I still have to go with you?" I asked.

"She just came in about five minutes ago, and yes, you are in the car already, so let's just go so we can come back soon," she said.

"Can we stop and get barbecue over at Mrs. Miner's on the way back, Mama?" I asked.

"I don't see why not. That's a good idea. Why don't you ask your daddy if it's okay. He may be able to get Quarter to give us some pork skin."

"Oh, Mama, I almost forgot. Miss Mass wants you to save her some cantaloupes, about two or three, 'cause she wants to give them to Mrs. Rita Portheng."

"Who is Rita Portheng?" asked Mama, frowning her brow at me.

"I don't know. Miss Mass says she lives out at Anderson's Nursing Home."

"Oooh!" Mama said, laughing out loud. "You talking about Rita Morgan. Mrs. Morgan, her son died not so long ago." Mama continued to laugh.

"What's so funny, Kate?" Dah asked as he opened the driver's-side door and sat behind the wheel.

Mama couldn't catch her breath from laughter. "Brown, you know how Miss Mass talks and run her words together?"

"Yeah," Dah said.

"Well, she asked Hundey to give me a message to save her some cantaloupes for Mrs. Rita, and Miss Mass must have referred to 'Mrs. Rita, poor thing,' and your daughter thought it was the woman's last name. Lord, girl, you gon' make me laugh till I break my water."

Dah let out a chuckle. "Well, Miss Mass can say some funny things sometimes, that's for sho'."

Ben came out of the house, wearing a T-shirt and blue jeans. Dah asked him if he wanted to drive, 'cause he was tired of driving. "Been driving straight for two days almost, and I am wore out. Kate, why don't you get in the back with Big Gal so I can sit up here with Maine."

Sometimes Dah called me Big Gal when he was relaxed. He gave me that nickname, and only he called me that. I didn't like it because it made me feel conscious of my size. I may have weighed 105 pounds, but the adults said that I had big bones and that was what made me look larger than what I was.

Our cotton and vegetable fields weren't far. A short drive or about a twenty-minute walk from our home. Mama got out of the front seat and sat in the back with me just as the house phone started to ring. "I got it!" I said, jumping out of the car and stepping up on the porch. I grabbed the phone quickly. "Hello, Browns' residence."

A familiar voice said, "Hello, may I speak with your mother, please? This is Mrs. Nichols. Can you go get her for me?"

I responded with a lie. "Hello, ma'am, this is Willie Mae. Mama is not here at the moment. She just left with my father and will be back about five tonight. May I help you?" I asked.

"Yes, you can," she said. "Please ask her to call me back tomorrow, I would say before ten in the morning. Tell her I've been waiting on her call. Now repeat what I told you back to me," she asked.

I did so.

"Well," she said, "I'm impressed, Willie Mae. That's exactly right. Thank you and bye-bye." She hung up.

I was so excited. I knew I had the job now. I just had to convince Mama to convince Dah. I spun around in the living room, happy as could be, and crashed right into Lou standing in the doorway.

"You lied to that person on the phone. Mama is right outside in the car. Why you told her what you did? Why, Hundey? Who was that?" she asked.

Dah blew the horn and the phone rang again.

Lou and I looked at each other. She answered the phone and took a message from my aunt Susta. Then Lou brushed past me and went out to the car to give Mama the message. I followed her, so afraid she was going to tell on me. I didn't say a word.

Mama never asked who the first caller was, and Lou never told her. I was relieved for the moment, but I had lied to the woman. Mama didn't like lies. She often said that if you lie, you'll steal. They went hand in hand.

When we got to the sweet potato field, Dah had all of us walk a few rows of potatoes and pull up some weeds and vines as he hoed around them. I took this opportunity to plot my story to Mama. She was walking a bit farther up a row, so it gave me time to think how I would explain my actions to her. I knew what to do. I would tell her the truth. I would say, "Mama, you didn't ask me who called the first time the phone rang." And when she said, "Well, who did call?" I would say, "Mrs. Nichols." Then that's when I would tell her that I didn't want Daddy to know that I was going to work for a white woman. That was it. That was what I would say.

So I started running up the rows as fast as I could in the dirt and caught up with her. She had almost made it to the little stream that ran across the land, the one Dah called a "soft spot." The dirt at the soft spot was full of minerals and white in color with an unusual smell like sulfur, and the soft spot always looked like it was fizzing. Some of the women in the country ate the dirt around these soft spots, especially the pregnant women, who called it "sour dirt." When a section of it was discovered, you could see women gather and hunch over the mound, twisting metal spoons into the earth, scooping out the dirt, and depositing it into brown paper bags. Mama said it tasted good and that her mother had eaten it when she was growing up.

I watched as Mama found a small mound and began excavating. She spooned out the dirt in round lumps and cupped them in her handkerchief while beckoning me to come over to her. "This dirt is fizzing, bubbling, with

nature's minerals," she yelled. "I tasted it and it is ripe."
She wanted me to have a taste, which I had refused many
times before.

I wanted to please her today, so I took the whitish lump
from her hand and put it on my tongue. I almost gagged
and immediately expelled the grit from the compound in
a lump of spit. My whole countenance was offended. I
shook my head and grimaced.

"Why you spitted it out, girl?" she asked, frowning.

"I don't like it!" I said, wiping my tongue with the hem
of my shirt. With the grit still floating on my tongue, I
questioned Mama through the cleansing. "Mama, do you
think I can work for that woman who called you today, I
mean yesterday?" I asked, hoping she didn't catch the slip.

Yet Mama did, and she asked, "Who's been calling on
that phone?"

I replied, "That was Mrs. Nichols, but we were about
to leave, so I didn't come for you."

Mama stood up from scooping the dirt. "Y'all keep
forgetting that I was a child before." She never turned to
face me. "And children think sometimes they are smarter
than grown folk. But let me say this to you, Hundey. I
didn't get this far being a fool, so I hope you stop playing
with me, and very soon, if I may add. Now you know
what I'm going to do?"

"No'm. I don't know what you gonna do. Are you

gonna punish me?" I asked with my finger in my mouth, trying to get out more of the nasty grit.

"Nawh, I ain't gonna punish you. I am going to let you go to work for that woman against your daddy's knowledge and let you see what it's like to be on your own. Now, when you start to work, don't ask me for any money. You keep what you make and buy what you need for school. I will get your clothes and shoes 'cause she's not going to pay you that much. That will save me more money to buy for the others. I am going to watch you now. 'Member that!" she said, facing me. "I'll take care of your daddy."

We moved away from the field and walked slowly behind Maine and Dah. Dah seemed content as he walked long strides ahead of us, looking above at the sky, walking the rows and admiring his crop. "Old Credo does some good work, now don't he, Maine?"

Maine agreed. "Yes, sir."

"What y'all want to do now?" Dah asked.

"We want to go to Mrs. Miner's and get some barbecue and potato salad, fo' it gits too crowded, Brown, if you don't mind," said Mama.

"All right then, let's go over to Mrs. Miner's to pick up some dinner. Looks like it's going to open up any minute. Them clouds up there look very dark and heavy."

Dah urged us to get into the car and instructed Maine to drive. "Maine, you get behind the wheel. I want to sit here and stretch my legs. Been driving for days and that 'quipment they using now is heavy. Summa it weigh a ton," he said, hiking up his pants and tucking in his shirt. He took the car keys out of his front pocket and handed them to Maine. Then he reached into his back pocket, pulled out a small pint of gin, uncapped it, and pressed the head of the bottle to his lips. The hand holding the bottle trembled as he took a swig. "Aah yak!" he said loudly as the liquor made its hot descent down his throat. He put the cap on the gin bottle. "Umph! That's it, y'all. Let's go."

Mama was frowning, disappointed that Dah had taken the hit of liquor.

"Now, Kate, when we git down there to Mrs. Miner's, I'm going to the back of the kitchen, back there to find Quarter." Quarter was Mrs. Miner's son. "He owes me a little change from a while ago, so you and the kids order what you want and I'll pay for it," he said, wiping the back of his hand across his wet mouth and pushing the bottle into his back pocket. "And, Maine, when they get the food, you take them home and come right back to git me. Don't even pull up in the yard. Hear me?"

Maine answered, "Yessir."

"Yeah, you just come right back 'cause I don't want your mama carryin' on 'bout me bein' out here too long. You know what I mean."

"Okay, okay, Dah. I'll be back for you real quick."

While Maine sat in the car with Chauncey and Noon-chi, Dah disappeared to the yard out back next to the barbecue pit, where men liked to gather. I followed Dah and peeked around back. From where I was standing there was lots of hand shaking as patrons and friends approached the pit. Half of a pig carcass slowly turned to a crispy piece of sizzling meat. Mostly men gathered to converse, while most of the women chose to remain inside the small café, protecting newly washed and pressed, curled hair.

I went inside. There were not many chairs to sit in, so Mama and I stood at the café counter, waiting for food. Because we had gotten there early, our wait was short. The owner came in, carrying a fresh pan of fried fish. Mama immediately ordered some to take home with us on top of the barbecue and other things we'd ordered.

"Mrs. Miner, you look good. How you been these days, with your hair so pretty, piled up on your head like that?" Mama asked, greeting Mrs. Miner with a smile.

"Katie, this here hair needs washing bad, but thank you anyway! Now which one of them children is this pretty one?" she asked, putting the pan on the counter and motioning for someone in the back to come for it. She wiped her hands on her soiled apron then reached down and grabbed my face with one of her hands. Holding my jaws tightly, she said, "Why she so pretty, Kate? An' ain't got nary a bump or blackhead in her face. An' them teeth! White as can be, like the clouds in the sky out there right now. And you know we 'specting rain," she said, looking up at Mama. "How old is she? How old you is, baby?" she asked me and Mama, still squeezing my face and looking me over like I was for sale.

Before Mama could answer, Mrs. Miner reached in her apron pocket and pulled out a pork rind, which she placed in my mouth. Mama graciously took her handkerchief out of her shirt pocket and removed the rind from my mouth and Mrs. Miner's hand from around my chin. "Don't want her to git too use to them thangs, Mrs. Miner," Mama said, whispering. "Fo' you know it, she'll be out there in the sto' every minute looking for 'em. She still a child, you know, and sugar runs in the family, on her daddy side. Plus them kinna thangs make 'em wormy and constipated. You know what I mean," Mama explained to her in a soft voice, trying not to make her feel bad.

Mrs. Miner laughed. "Oh, Katie, that ain't nuthin but a piece of rind. My chillren's brought up on that stuff and ain't na'un of 'em ever been sick buhind eatin' them. But you right 'bout watching out for 'em. I don't blame you. Next time you come, brang that other daughter wit you. I'd love to see her, too. Susta's got some clothes she done grown outta that may fit her." All these words she spoke seemed to run together, and in a flash she had gone out the screen door.

I was so happy to be released from her hand's grip around my mouth, 'cause it seemed like my jaws had clamped together and it hurt.

"Shoot! If I had asked her one time, I've asked her twice not to put thangs in y'all mouths, and she do the same thang every time I come in here wit one of y'all." Mama was frustrated and she had put her right foot up on her left shin, standing there like a Florida pink bird. "And the nerve of her to offer me some of her daughter's clothes for your sister when people right here in this area need them." Mama used the handkerchief to dab her face.

Our dinner order came out, carried by Quarter himself. "Mrs. Brown! Mrs. Brown, how you doing today, Mrs. Brown? I ain't seen you in a lonnng time," he said, dragging out the word. "You been all right?"

"Yeah, I've been good, Quarter. I see you done put a little mustache on your face. It becomes you. How much you got for me?" she asked, untying her handkerchief to remove the paper money.

"Uhhh. No!" said Quarter, holding up his hands to stop her. "Me and Brown done already figured this out. We squared away now. Put it back in your pocket, and I

added a few more pieces of fish to it. How about that!"
he said, not waiting for a reply.

"And which one is this here with you today?" he asked,
smiling at me as he packed the bags.

I moved closer to Mama and put my hand over my
mouth.

"Is this here Big Girl I hear Mr. Brown brag about?"

"My name is Willie Mae."

"Well, okay, Willie Mae, you be a good girl, and take
care, Mrs. Brown. I'm going back out here with Mr. Brown.
Y'all take care." Quarter left quickly out the back screen
door, letting it flap its way shut as the pork smoke from
the barbecue pit sifted its way through the torn screen.

Ben appeared to help us carry out our food and he
drove us home. Lou joined the rest of us at the table with
the greasy paper bags balled up around us. And then the
meal unfolded like the delicious ritual it always was.

The pork barbecue aroma lit up the house with its
smoky smell, and Mrs. Miner's hot sauce added a savory
scent. The bread was soft and lightly soaked in the steam
and oil from the fillets, perfect for fish sandwiches. The
Cokes were ice-cold, just right to douse out a mouth on
fire 'cause you were too hungry for the food to cool, and
blowing on it just made you mo' hungrier than you was.
After a bite, circular mouths blew out overheated air,

and hands fanned faces flushed from steam. As the food cooled and started disappearing, we laughed and talked about the day, picked smaller fish bones off the back of our tongues, and then one of us snatched a bite of fish from someone else's plate when they wasn't looking.

"What, what you staring at me for? I didn't do nothing."

"I didn't say you did anything. I was just looking. What you guilty of?"

"Someone guilty 'cause someone broke off a piece of yo' fish while you weren't looking."

The fish robber looked down and sniggered, and the victim bit into an empty piece of bread. Everybody laughed.

"You better gimme back my fish fo' I take all yours!" the victim demanded.

"Noooo! Don't touch my plate! Mama, tell 'em not to touch my plate!" said the thief, jumping up with their plate and hiding behind Mama.

More laughter.

"Okay, that's enough," said Mama. "Y'all stop that and YOU . . . go sit down with that plate and finish eating. Y'all be quiet now and eat!"

The thief sat down, still guarding the plate. The sniggering turned into laughter, and then somebody started gagging. Everything stopped. Half-eaten fish sandwiches were frozen in motionless hands, eyes locked on the choking one. Nobody spoke.

Mama jumped up. "Spit it out!" she yelled. "Spit it right out in my hand. You done got hold a fish bone, probably a thin one from the way you sound." By then, Mama had her hand down one of our throats and she was fishing for the bone. More gagging. "Go in that icebox quick and get me a lemon !" she cried. The lemon would dry up some of the mucus in the mouth and allow her to get a grip on the small bone.

Someone then moved quickly to assist Mama, and she squeezed some juice on her hand and somehow got the bone out. Everyone had stopped eating till it was over and she had cleaned up the table and washed the face of the assaulted one.

"I forgot to pick the bones out of that piece before you started eating it," Mama said quietly, rubbing her hand over the shaken one's face, which was her way of apologizing to us. "Move over there," she said to the person near her. "Let that baby sit by me so I can watch how she picks out these bones." Whoever was near jumped up and gave our sibling the chair. We waited until the assaulted one was safe, and we resumed talking.

After dinner Ben announced that he was going to get Dah. I was ready to ask Mama about what she had said in the field earlier.

"Can I really work for Mrs. Nichols?" I asked her, and she said yes, she was going to let me try working for a week, starting in three days. I was so happy and so satisfied at her just saying yes. I thought for sure it was going to be a big fat "No, and don't ask me anymore!"

In fact, I was so happy that I did the dishes before I was told, and I mopped the floor. I must have gone over the floor twice before hearing Mama say, "Put that mop down, Hundey, and go get cleaned up for bed!"

That's just where I wanted to be, in bed on those white West Point sheets with the lights off so that I could dream up the money and freedom I was going to have by working. I thought about the two children that Mrs. Nichols had and how they would look, how they would act. Were they good children, or was she mean and hiding it? Was she a Christian? I wanted to also see into her closet and go through her clothes, smell her air, which would reveal her true nature to me. I certainly hoped she was nice and had a color TV and a nice clean home like mine.

The day couldn't come fast enough. It was like waiting on a holiday.

Growing Up in Selma

1.

Mrs. Nichols called Mama a few more times before I started working for her at the trailer court. Yes, she lived in a wide-body trailer with three bedrooms and one and a half baths. The little girl's room was done in lace with pink walls, a matching bedspread, and cute dolls. The boy's room was bunk beds against the wall, and brown-and-beige wallpaper with cowboys and Western designs on the sheets and bedspreads—and I sniffed the smell of pee.

The children were sweet, with sunny faces and freckled noses, blue eyes and platinum hair. I sensed the five-year-old girl was her favorite. The boy, four, Mrs. Nichols warned me on my first day, "he doesn't listen." I liked them both, and they liked me.

Peggy Nichols was attractive, with beautiful full legs and a size twelve, perfect Coca-Cola figure, bleached blond hair, blue eyes, and not-so-thin lips. She worked the day shift at the bar out on Highway 14, the Pen. WHITE ONLY! said the sign on the door.

Mrs. Nichols was a divorcée, Noonchi had told me, dating a married man who built bridges and gave her money. I found this fascinating. There was something inside of me that was most curious about the lives of grown folks. They intrigued me, all of them, because they carried secrets. They carried pain in their faces or in their hands. They spoke their minds as though they were preaching, repeating sentences with emphasis on certain words to enhance what they were trying to convey.

Grown folk watched other grown folk carefully, Negroes or whites. But they listened to each other differently. If whites were engrossed in listening to what a Negro was saying to them, they might make a scornful face or raise an eyebrow, or fix their mouth and nose like they were smelling something unpleasant. Negroes listened to whites with downcast eyes or lowered heads.

I had yet to meet Cole, the boyfriend, but I knew he was another woman's husband, having snuck a peek at some of his letters to Peggy that I had seen lying on her dresser. Hastily ripped-open envelopes suggested her excitement at reading the words that could possibly massage her aching heart and reduce the flashes of heat running through her body for the moment. A bold one, Cole was, with a sneaky demeanor. He went straight to the point with *I love YOU*. Categorizing her apart from his legalized and biological responsibilities, he underscored *YOU* with fierce repeated lines yet was merciless in the conclusion of the letter. *I am NOT leaving home anytime soon*, he wrote with confidence and fearlessness in his delivery, because he knew she loved him and needed him.

Mrs. Nichols could have had nearly any white man in Selma. She made money, mostly in tips, and she was very attractive, a typical blond beauty who drove a brand-new red-and-white convertible, courtesy of Cole. She paid me twenty-five dollars a week and said I could eat anything I wanted in her fridge and take a nap when her young'uns did.

She called home often to check on them as well as to check on me. My mother, or one of my siblings, called to check on me also. I worked about nine hours a day. I felt like I was having lots of fun. However, after about three weeks of working for her, I was eager to take off some time to be with my family and friends. But I had nothing to do and nothing to wear going out with my friends. I went into her closet, took one look at a tweed blazer, and decided to borrow it without asking her.

Mrs. Nichols brought me home that afternoon, and I rushed out of her car with the jacket inside the grip I'd borrowed from Dah's closet. That evening when I wore it out to the neighborhood baseball game, I acted like it was all mine, accepting the compliments with grand lies about how I'd acquired it.

Later, however, I felt sickened by my actions. After I got home, I rushed directly to our bedroom, which was empty. I removed the jacket, hid it in the back of the closet, and fell into the first bed in there, Noonchi's. That was a bad choice, because she was known to have an open Baby Ruth candy bar under the pillow, and there was some peanuts and chocolate smeared all over her sheets. I got off and moved past Lou's bed, too, and jumped into the bed I shared with Chauncey, which was more comforting. Then I turned toward the window and cried, promising myself to return the jacket when I went back over there in a couple of days. I knew Peggy wouldn't miss the jacket because she had put it in the hallway closet, and the wardrobe she was using at the time was in her bedroom closet.

The next day I used some of my babysitting money

and had the garment cleaned, and when I went back to work, I secretly returned it to its rightful place.

2.

One day I finally met Cole after bringing the children home from the playground. I found him sitting cozily on the built-in sofa next to Mrs. Nichols, wearing a white T-shirt and dark slacks, holding a stump of a cigar. As she introduced him, I couldn't help staring at the band of gold that circled his ring finger and weighed down the hair around its knuckle. He spoke to me with dark eyes under a crown of shiny mink hair, which was coarser than the hair protruding out of the V-neck of his shirt. The tan on his skin was strikingly dark.

"Hey, you two!" he greeted the young'uns. They ran to him and hugged him tightly, their voices straining over each other for his attention. He put his hand into his pocket and gave them each a dollar bill, which lit up their faces, and they flew to their rooms to examine the money more closely. Cole stood up from the sofa and excused himself to "check around outside." He then went through the front door and down the steps.

Mrs. Nichols spoke to me. "Willie Mae, I will let your

mother know that Cole will be staying here for a while to help me out. He'll be here in my room most of the time, so if you hear someone coming in and out, it will be Cole. And if the door to my room is closed, please knock. If someone should come to the door, looking for Cole or me, roll out the trailer window and see who it is. Take a message and I'll take care of it later. Okay?" she asked.

I nodded yes.

Mrs. Nichols said that Cole would be working on a project in Selma for a few days. "Now, Willie Mae, you keep my kids quiet. I don't want them disturbing Cole, because I like having him here, and I would like to see more of him. Willie Mae, you are really taking good care of my kids, and I know how much they look forward to seeing you. Tonight I need you to stay over late and I will pay you an extra dollar this week. I'm going to speak with your mother later today. What you think about that?" she asked with a "proud of myself, look what I have done for you" attitude.

"I don't mind as long as my parents say okay," I said. I wasn't too happy about staying late, because I wanted to be around my family and friends. Dah was back on the road traveling with the railroad again, putting down crossties and tracks, so I didn't have him to think about. Mama and Maine were in charge of everything.

After Mrs. Nichols left that afternoon, I got a call from my sister Lou, telling me, "Mama wants you to come home and for me to watch Peggy's kids. Mama is sending me out in a cab and you are to return in the same car."

I was sort of relieved by the switch until I found out that Mama'd told Lou I'd have to give her ten dollars for the late night. Then I would only be getting sixteen dollars for the week. And Mama wanted me to contribute another ten dollars to the house 'cause Dah was not coming home as planned. That would leave me with six dollars for four days of sitting.

I couldn't argue with anyone, 'cause for one thing, I really liked helping and sharing, and I knew how good Mama was to all of us. She had never asked me to contribute anything to the house, so I felt big and proud to be helping out this week.

I came home that evening and handed Mama all my money just as I saw Dah do with his paycheck. Mama gave me six dollars and asked me to go get change for the five from Deak D'Ampars's store. Out of the five, she gave me four and explained that she was saving one dollar for me when I needed it most.

I felt good to be home early and with my family. We all had supper together and discussed the things we would do on Saturday. That night it had begun to drizzle outside, and we slept uninterrupted to the relaxing sounds of water on the roof.

3.

Early the next morning, the black Saturday sky opened up and the rain fell in sheets, drenching the roof of the house and the front porch. Everyone stayed inside. The cars traveling on the streets moved slowly or pulled over to allow the rain to pass. Thunder shook the house and lightning crackled at the windows. Telephone poles and clotheslines fell in yards, and stray cats and whimpering dogs ran for cover under houses to hide. The storm started before breakfast, around five o'clock in the morning, and we all stayed in bed while God did his work.

Noonchi was sound asleep, lightly snoring. "Lay still and stop all that talk, you two," Mama said to me and Lou from the doorway. So we put the covers over our heads and talked with the sheets up to our mouths so she wouldn't hear us.

The phone rang and Mama got up to answer it. "I'll call you back. It's lightning over here," she said to the caller, and hung up the telephone.

It must have poured rain for ten more minutes, and then it stopped suddenly and the sun split through the curtains in the bedrooms and burst through the drapes in the living room. We girls jumped up out of bed and ran to the bathroom door. It was occupied. Maine was in there, and the smell of Old Spice was floating in the air. We had only one bathroom, and we all had to go. "I'm gonna run over to the house next door," Noonchi said.

"No," said Mama. "You know that Joe and Bertha Mae and their daughter Baby Smiley are moving in today, so I don't want y'all using your spare key, going in and out of there anymore. They got some of their things up in there already, and I gave them the key. They gonna finish moving in sometime this evening," she said.

A fence separated our house from the smaller rental property next door. Our house was larger and painted white. The house next door was unfinished, with two bedrooms and a porch on the front and back. It was the color of driftwood and possibly had been used for the servants long ago who worked for the owners of the house we lived in. When we first moved in, the only thing in the unfinished house was a potbelly stove. Dah had added a bathroom and new windows.

"Maine, come out of that restroom. These children got to get in there. You been in there long enough now. Come on."

Maine finally came out the bathroom, all dressed up in blue dress pants and a white starched shirt.

Mama looked surprised. "Boy, where you think you going this time of morning with them Sunday church clothes on?"

Ben answered, "I am going over to East Selma to pick up Evelyn and take her and Mrs. White to the bus depot. Mrs. White is going to visit her aunt T in Virginia, and after we drop her off, we going down to the Circle-In Café and eat some breakfast. Is that okay?"

Mama replied, "That will be fine, Maine. But I want you to know that some of those white ministers eat in there sometimes. You keep to yourself. And you know you have to be back here to take me to Jean's at noon, don't you?"

"Yes, ma'am, I know. I'll be careful."

"And," said Mama, "I want you back here after that to make sure everything is going good with Bertha Mae." She kissed him on his cheek. "You sure look nice. Be sweet now."

"He don't look good," I said, picking at Ben and laughing. "He look like he going to work at the Cream Queen." I ran out the room giggling.

Later that morning, a truck with a load of furnishings and rugs thrown over the pile pulled up on the sidewalk in front of the house next door, and a very large round woman in a pretty dress and flat shoes got out of the cab of the truck and headed straight toward our house. The man driving the truck exited the driver's side, took out a bag of chewing tobacco, and put a pinch in his mouth. "B'der inna minnit, ba'y," he said to her.

The man walked up to the house and used his key to open the door. I saw the new shades Dah had installed in the living room go up, and I ran out to the front porch after Mama.

The woman had made her way to our house and taken a seat in one of the matching sun chairs on our porch next to Mama, smiling with a mouthful of bright pink gums and a brilliant gold crown on her eyetooth. Her smile was beautiful, and I liked the contrast right away. She smelled like fresh lemons and also sweat, which had pooled around the three rolls of flesh on her neck, leaving a glistening shine on her wet skin, covering part of a gold cross and the head of Jesus Christ. I knew it was Jesus 'cause I could see his crucified feet. When her head moved, Jesus's feet stayed in place, nailed to the cross and her chest.

Bertha was one of our favorite relatives. It had been years since we had seen her, but she kept in touch with postal letters. Because of Dah's work, it was difficult to visit them often. My mother didn't drive, and the trip to Choctaw County was long and they lived in the back-woods, surrounded by beautiful raw land.

"Aint Kate, I do pre-shate diss here y'all done did for me and my family. Joe is so glad to get out of Choctaw that he don't know what to do with hisself," she said, looking at Mama while holding her hands in her lap. "Kate, we ken finally see sum peoples 'stead of being cooped up in that place all the time, looking at red roads." She clapped her hands together and said out loud, "Selma! Lord looka here." Her mouth never relinquished the smile.

Then she turned to me. "Dis here Hundey, Aint Kate?" she asked.

"Yes, that's her," Mama said. "Go on over there and give Aunt Bertha a hug, and stop staring at her."

I walked over to her and stretched out my arms as wide as I could to give her a hug, and I made a grunting sound as if I was using all my strength. My head felt like it had fallen on a pillow as it lay on her stomach, my arms reaching only to the side of her apron pocket because they couldn't go any farther.

Aunt Bertha pulled me away from her and told me that her little girl Urmagene was on her way to Selma, and she was being driven here because there was no room in the truck. "You and Baby Smiley gon' have lots of fun together. She just loves being wit' girls her own age and the right thang about it is, both of y'all related, now don't that beat all! Hallelujah, Jesus," she added, still grinning and talking. "I nicknamed her Ba'y Smiley 'cause she smile so much. When she was a real little girl, nothing made that baby cry. She could drop a candy sucker from her mouth and onto the ground, and she would pick it up and hand it to me with a smile on her face. Most chillren would have a fit. Ain't that right, Kate?"

With lips slightly pursed, Mama gave a small nod in agreement.

"So we nicknamed her Ba'y Smiley," Bertha said with tenderness. There was silence for a moment, and we all stared out at the traffic.

Mama spoke: "So you and Joe going to unpack for the rest of the day and settle down around time for supper? Or what y'all going to do?"

"Uh-huh, that's pretty much it for the day," Bertha said. "Y'all cleaned the house for us real nice and we grateful. The yard looks nice, too, so it's just putting stuff away right now. We brought some food from home, and our clothes are coming this afternoon with my daughter."

As she got up to go, Bertha said, "Ever'body doing well at home, Kate. They all have jobs doing work for somebody regularly, anythang to git by, and ever'body's in the church, by the grace of God. You know we can't prosper none without Him. He the way maker, sho'nuf," she said, as Mama said "Amen" softly.

We watched her walk across the yard and through the gate between our yards. As she reached their porch, Joe came out of the house and smiled and waved to us. Then he went back to pulling furniture off the truck.

Maine returned after a while to take Mama and my sisters to Jean's. I didn't like it there because Jean lived too close to a cemetery, and, I swear to God, her house was haunted. Haints were always in there. Even in broad daylight. Especially when Jean made biscuits. Every time cousin Jean made biscuits, a thin, dark-skinned woman seemed to appear in the kitchen and stand near the stove, staring at Jean while she rolled out dough with a glass. I saw this with my own eyes.

One time when I was very young, cousin Jean couldn't find the tall drinking glass she used to roll the dough, so she dug out a proper rolling pin from the back of a cabinet to use. And God may kill me if I lie, but you would have thought a freight train came into the house. Cabinet doors started shaking and knickknacks on the coffee table trembled and moved. The screen door slammed shut and lots of things fell off the tables. Mama had two of us with her that day, and my little sister Chauncey was a baby at the time. Mama did something I had never seen before. She grabbed up the baby and woke her up and stuck her titty in the baby's mouth after she had skeeted some breast milk on the floor to calm the haint. Things stopped, and Mama urged Jean to clean her house and put a new coat of paint in each room. "Jeannie, you got to get rid of them thangs. They coming out of that cemetery ovah there and it's gon' take a toll on you if you don't," said Mama.

"Aunt Kate, Lord knows I have prayed 'bout this for a long time, and I b'lieve this house has got to go. A woman that use ta live here had a lot of family members that passed right in these rooms, and I don't thank they had good deaths. We planning on moving soon anyway, going to Bessemer is what Charles want to do."

Then Mama and Jean acted like nothing out of the ordinary had happened, like it was normal. They continued talking as if the visitor was a human being and not a so-called spirit. Jean said that sometimes she would glimpse the haint in the kitchen when she was cooking. And "maybe" when she used something different to make the bread, which seemed to disturb the haint.

That day, I went out to the front porch and stayed there till Maine came to get us. I never wanted to go there again, and I expressed this to Mama on the way home. "Mama, I am scared to be there, because that house ain't right and them haints! I can see them and feel them," I said.

"Oh, stop it!" said Mama. "Ain't that bad."

"Then why you skeet that milk onto the floor?" I asked her.

"Just in case," she replied. "Just in case."

Sometimes in Selma, it would rain as the sun was shining brightly. My mama often said that when this happened, it was because the devil was beating his wife. What nonsense, I had thought. Maybe the devil's wife was crying out of boredom, something I felt like doing. After I had finished my chores and put a hem in the dress I would wear to church the next day, there was nothing to do. Sitting on the front porch alone, I watched more rain clouds take over the sky.

I must've fallen asleep in the sun chair and was awakened by hearing Maine through the window talking on the phone in Dah's room. He stayed on the phone with somebody all the time. I couldn't make out what he was saying, so I got up and went off around to the side of the house where the dogs were kept and turned the hose pipe on to wash out their bowls and give them fresh, cool water, then watched as they lapped it up. The dogs wanted me to pet and play with them, but I couldn't. They were hunting dogs, and they could bite me really badly.

Maine yelled out the window for me to leave them alone.

I responded by saying, "I just wanted to give them water!"

He told me to "go introduce yourself to your cousin in the rented house." That was an idea. I would wash my hands and pull my hair back and go over there to meet my cousin, my new friend, Baby Smiley.

Ten minutes later I was knocking on the door and heard my aunt say, "Come on in. We here in the back."

I walked into the living room, where Aunt Bertha

had transformed the house into a cute little cottage and arranged a group of three very comfortable sitting chairs with embroidered bouquets of flowers on the cushions next to a two-seat divan and three standing lamps with shades. A circular rug covered most of the floor. On the walls hung pictures of people whom I had never seen before. The white shades Dah had put on the windows throughout the house were now covered with heavy lace curtains. A large brown wooden cabinet held a radio and a bowl of hard candy. Dah had cleaned out the chimney and fireplace a few weeks prior. Joe had already chopped some logs and stacked them up beside the grate in preparation for the cold winter ahead. I was impressed.

"We in the kitchen," Aunt Bertha called out again. This was a small house but it seemed so big suddenly.

"Yes, ma'am. It's me, Hundey," I said, walking toward the kitchen. I was stopped cold, never making it through the doorway. It wasn't that the dining area had been transformed, with a small table and stuffed chairs around it. No. It wasn't the powerful presence of a quaint home with family. What it was, was a miniature twin of Aunt Bertha, sitting on the floor with a comic. Their figures, the shape of their faces, were identical. But unlike Aunt Bertha, the girl had a very dark complexion, like her father's. She also had startling golden eyes, and her gums were darker and low because she had short teeth. Her hair was almost the color of her eyes. I had never seen this strange beauty before, and it was confusing. Different.

I stared at the girl, then at Joe and Bertha. They were staring at me with smiling faces.

"Git up, Ba'y," Joe said to the sandy-brown-haired girl with his brow furrowed. "Git up and give your relation a hug. Where's yo' manners?"

The mother stood back, proud, with a sunny wide smile on her face and a mixing spoon in her hand. The girl rolled over to one side of the floor, jumped up fast, and ran over to hug me. She wrapped her arms around my whole body and then stepped back, her body jiggling.

"What cho' name?" she asked with a lisp, rounded front teeth, no smile, breathing hard, chewing on something, possibly gristle, because she smelled like Florida Water and chicken. "What cho' name?" she asked me again, and I heard her mother say, "It's Willie Mae, but don't call her that. Call her Hundey. I thank she just shamed shy-faced right now, that's all. She gon' get used to us soon. Wait till y'all start playing."

I made an excuse right away. "I just came by to say hey. I have to get back now." I waved bye to them, then quickly left the room and rushed out of the house.

When I got to the front door, I ran back to Dah's room. Maine was still on the phone. I yelled at him to "Get off the phone now!"

I couldn't breathe.

Ben put his hand over the mouthpiece. "What's wrong with you?" he yelled. "Hey, lemme call you back. Something has happened to Willie Mae." He put the phone down. "Hundey, what happened? What's wrong? Tell me, please."

I started to cry, and then I started to laugh.

"Oh, Jesus. I done let somebody hurt you?" He ran to the kitchen for some water.

When he came back, I told him to go over to the other house and take notice of those people.

"Why?" he asked. "What's wrong with them?"

"Just go look at them carefully and come back and tell me what you see. I demand it!"

So Ben walked over to the house and came back home shortly. He sat down on the porch with me and began to laugh, and we laughed together. Ben started patting his foot as he spoke in slow pauses. "They are real clean. Real nice, and real country people . . . and ahhhh . . . Urmagene looks just like her mother. Exactly like her, and they don't stop laughing and talking, and Urmagene doesn't smile. She and her daddy are dark-skinned also, and Urmagene has sandy-brown hair and gold eyes, and you don't relate to them because they don't look like you. Is that what scared you?" he asked me.

I started to cry again and asked him to call Mama to

come home. He did, and we went out to the haunted house to get her. I rode in the back seat alone.

Mama came out the house just as we drove up, and got into the back seat of the car with me when she saw my sad face. As we drove, Maine told her what was going on.

Mama took one look at me and told me that I needed to stop looking so deep into people's lives. That I was seeing too much, probing too hard, and "creating too much chaos for my mind." She told me that I needed to turn off my wondering and visions, deny the spirit of the vision when it was coming, when I felt it. "You get too involved in it. You get that from my side of the family. My grandmother was like you. After a while, she didn't want to even meet anybody and spoke to people with her head down, not to be impolite, but just to be safe. Hundey, you too young to be like that. Just stop looking too deeply inside." Then she put her hand in mine and said to me, "You all right, child. Don't worry."

4.

Our new neighbors next door took to stopping by for short visits. Joe was very kind—and helpful when Dah was gone. He cut our grass without being asked. He went out to the fields with Maine to help weed out the rows. Aunt Bertha cooked and baked cakes as a business, selling plates of food for four dollars a dinner and two dollars for a fish sandwich and a pickle on Saturdays. Many people didn't want to cook on the weekends, and Aunt Bertha's business could make good money on those days. Two days a week, Aunt Bertha went to work for a lawyer down on Dallas Avenue and cooked for his family, bringing home their leftovers for her family.

It seemed Urmagene and I were becoming friends just by spending time together at each other's houses those first few days. She had come to play ball with me and my friends once in the vacant lot, and my friends had become her friends. We were together often.

Other times we just kept quiet on the porch and looked through magazines and the funny papers. Urmagene liked to stretch out on the porch with the funny papers, and she used the older ones to cover the walls in her bedroom. I liked the *Jet* magazines because they showed all the beautiful Negro people in the world, where they traveled, what they saw, how they dressed, and all their problems and progress living in America. Dah subscribed to the magazines for us to keep up with the civil rights issues. When he ordered *Jet*, he also had the *Selma Times-Journal* delivered to our house every morning.

Johnny Mann was the paperboy who delivered the *Selma Times* to homes on his old bicycle. He rode by fast, pitching the newspapers onto the front porches so they'd snap against the screen doors. *Flamp!* When we heard that noise, we knew what time it was because Johnny was never late.

The only time I remember him being late was when his grandma died, and he was only about ten minutes late then. Johnny's mama had been dead for a while, and his daddy was nowhere around. It was just him, his grand-daddy, and his sister left. He worked even on that sad day, riding through Selma, throwing them newspapers, his face streaming with tears and him crying his grandma's name out loud.

"Muhd-dear! Muhd-dear! Muhd-dear! Oh, Muhd-dear!"

Johnny Mann delivered papers in the white neighbor-hoods only in emergencies, 'cause we weren't allowed over there, but the day Mrs. Ginny Bee, who was his dear grandmother, his Muhd-dear, died, they said he'd picked up more papers than he was supposed to and rolled through the whole town of Selma, crying out her name and waking up everybody. That was his way of mourn-ing. At first, the white folks and even the law tried to get him to stop, but they said he was too fast on his bike and he wouldn't listen anyway. Neighborhood people started calling each other, spreading the news of Johnny's grand-mother's death. Neighbors expecting their papers stood still in glass picture windows or in yards, waiting to hear his cries. A police car finally caught up with the paperboy and trailed him throuhout Selma, lights flashing, maybe in sympathy, maybe cautionary. And Johnny never got arrested for trespassing.

I told Urmagene about this, but she didn't seem that interested. We didn't really talk much, and I got used to that. One day on the porch I told her, "Urmagene, I like that you read quietly."

I was expecting her to pay me a little compliment in return, but she didn't.

Instead, she shocked me by asking what had been wrong with me that first day I met her, when I up and left her house suddenly. She asked me if I was really shame-faced or just uppity, 'cause to her, it seemed I was being uppity.

I asked her what she meant by *uppity*, as if I didn't know.

"'Uppity' means maybe you think you better than somebody else."

"Urmagene, I don't think that way. That's all in your mind. I don't know what's wrong with you, but we were not taught to look down on people."

That's when Urmagene put down the funny papers and climbed up in the porch swing with me.

"Well," she said, "in case you do!" *Bam!* And she elbowed me hard in my right side, knocking my wind out.

As I folded in shock, gasping for breath, she stood

up and said, "Case you do think that, you ain't, and I am better than you and your whole family any day. Your mamm' came over here the other night and ask my mama did anything happen the other day. So what you tell her? Huh?" she demanded firmly.

"I didn't say nothing about you." Tears formed in my eyes. "I just said y'all were different-looking, more than a lot of people, and I wanted to know where did y'all get your looks. My mama told me that all people are different, and some Negroes are blacker than others and some are lighter than others." I was crying now. "Why did you punch me, Urmagene?" I asked, holding my stomach. "I've never hit you, and I thought we were friends. And we are cousins. And besides all that, there's lots of things that I don't know yet, and there are things I haven't seen yet. There are things that bother me that may not bother you."

She didn't respond right away but stood up from her seat in the midst of me crying and gasping and said, "Lots of people make fun of me 'cause I am real dark, 'specially crackers. Chillren mostly, who learnt this mess from they mamas and daddies. Colored folk kids do it also. The light-skinned colored ones wif good hair, they bad about it. So I been thinking you was thinking like that when you up and ran home, that I'm some big joke to you, not that you were shamefaced." And she ended the sentence by nonchalantly adding, "Sorry." She walked off the porch, popping bubble gum, heading back to her house like nothing happened.

I remained bent over in the swing, hearing her footsteps as she walked away. Sitting up slowly to avoid the pain, I wiped my eyes on the sleeve of my shirt. I couldn't get what had just happened out of my mind. No matter what, I knew she'd had no right to hit me. But I didn't know what I was going to do about it.

I was still thinking about it the next day, Sunday, when we all went down to Orrville to John the Baptist Church and then visited Dah's sister and family. It was beautiful country, with graying barns and luscious cow pastures. Usually I loved to play with my cousins. Sneaking through woods where we weren't supposed to be, we saw eagles in towering trees and buzzards circling the deep, dense forest, looking for carcasses. We knew where to go and had to learn to be patient in the woods. That way the woods would open up and allow us to explore their clearings, where we found sweet, cold, clear water moving through rocky gullies, but only if you knew where to go and weren't afraid of snakes. My cousins and I were not afraid of snakes and small animals. We were fond of picking and eating blackberries together in open fields among slate tombstones lying down and laced in greening moss, covering letters and names and numbers of the dead. It was us who found and identified them and tore back the moss, which allowed them to see the land again through their names.

This Sunday, our visit was not long, and we were home in time to have supper at our own house. In the car ride home I was quiet and thought about the sermon that Reverend Blevins had preached earlier.

It was about sinning. I kept hearing in my mind his words about turning the other cheek and not retaliating against someone who had harmed us. I was feeling trapped because Urmagene had hurt me, and now God was instructing me through my pastor to forgive and forget, to be friends with my cousin again and let it go. On the other hand, I knew that God helped those who helped themselves, and I didn't want to look like a punk. Somewhere, I had heard that Christ Jesus was not a punk. Well, I was going to turn the other cheek by taking my best shot right in her face on her cheek. That was my application to turn the other cheek, with my fist. The nerve she had, to hit me like that.

5.

Lou had been working for me at Mrs. Nichols's house for two days, and I was going back to work in a few more days to resume babysitting. Dah came home and never found out about my reaction to meeting Urmagene's family. He didn't even know about Lou and me working for Peggy Nichols. I don't think Mama had ever mentioned it to him.

I had told Maine what had happened with Urmagene. I wanted him to teach me how to fight. No one was going to do that to me again and get away with it.

"The only thing I can tell you to do is to get mad," he said as he made me come to the backyard with him when he and I were alone at the house one afternoon. "When you get really mad, you can kill someone, but that's not what I want you to do. Hold up your hands as high as you can. Now, I'm going to hit at you. Try to get out of my way or duck when you see the blow coming."

I was doing what he asked. He kept hitting me, and then I ducked when I saw the next blow coming. He caught my face once and I got angry. When he realized I was mad, he started to taunt me. "Come on, you high yellow gal, hit me. You can't hit because you got too much cracker in you. Hit me!" he demanded. I was mad now, and soon my fists were balled up, punching my brother like a wild person.

"Whoa now! Whoa now! Baby girl, you 'member I said don't kill nobody. You 'bout to kill your brother. I know you mad, but you need to save that for that cousin o' yourn. Come on, let's go get something to eat. Do you want to go to the Cream Queen for some food?" he asked.

"Okay," I said. "Just let me go in and clean myself up. Ah' right?"

"No, you don't need to do nothing like that. Just come on. Don't worry about the door being locked. It ain't nobody coming up in here, trust me. Let's ride," he said, as he hustled me to the car. After rolling down all the windows and turning up the music, he pulled out. "Act like you with me and do what you like. Look tough, 'cause you riding with Pop Brown and all the suckers know who I am. Just don't tell Mama, okay?"

I agreed.

When we drove up to the Cream Queen, Ben's friend Lawrence came up to wait on us. Lawrence's father owned the place, and Lawrence and Ben were very close friends. "Ben Brown! My man! What's going on, Ben? You got your little sister with you. That's nice," he said, staring at me. "You'll be in Hudson High School soon, right? Are you excited?" He was being nice, making conversation.

"I am excited," I answered.

"Hey, Lawrence, man, bring us two hamburgers and two chocolate milkshakes, and if you can get that quick, man, that will be good. I got to take my little sister home before dark."

"Okay, man. I'll bring that out right now."

I felt so good being with my big brother and meeting his friend. Usually he wasn't home, and when he was, he was on his way to help Dah in the field or go out with his girlfriend. I was beginning to feel better, and the sting from Ben's boxing wasn't hurting as much.

On the way home, Ben told me, "I didn't mean to hurt you, but when you get to fighting with Urmagene, she probably will hit you hard because she is strong and a big-ass country gal who has fought before. But don't be afraid and lose your breath. Don't let her hit you in the side or chest. Don't fear. Just tear her ass up, and if you have to put her face in the dirt, do it. Just don't disfigure her or kill her, and after this fight here, you won't be scared no more. I promise you."

I listened to him carefully and tried to absorb everything that he told me, but he could see on my face how worried I was.

"Look," he said. "That fast-tail gal didn't have to hit you, but she did, because she wanted to. You gon' have to stand up for yourself, and ain't no better time than now. Whup her, and then 'pologize just like she did when she strutted her rump off this porch. That'll teach her a lesson or two."

"Okay," I said.

"You just let me know when you're ready and we'll make a plan."

I wished I could talk to Lou about it.

I sensed she knew that something was going on because I caught her rolling her eyes my way when she passed me in the hallway. But I wasn't going to tell her anything about Urmagene, because Lou never wanted to tell me anything about her boyfriend or her plans. She had even stopped playing with me like she used to. We were pretty close in age and once had lots of fun.

Lou loved to dance the waltz and the two-step. I loved the turn in the two-step dance and how we would practice for hours. Time would fly by as we were having such fun. I recall the time Lou and her boyfriend Randy were chosen to be the king and queen of the freshman prom, and Lou wanted to practice with me so that she would be ready when she and Randy were called to the dance floor to give the first dance in the auditorium.

We practiced mostly as we cleaned our home on weekends. The radio was our source for music. We had to wait for a fast song to play on the radio before we could dance. The disc jockey was known to play three fast songs followed by three slow songs. We would clean as quickly as we could during the slow songs so that we could dance on all three fast ones.

If I was cleaning in the back room and Lou was in the living room where the radio was and a song was playing that we liked, I would hasten down the hallway with a dustrag in my skirt pocket and grab my partner. Some-times we messed up, missed a step or tripped. It didn't matter. We kept swinging in our gathered skirts, which were made by a seamstress in the neighborhood. The skirts had lots of material, which made them blow up when I was spun around. The double turn was the best. It made me laugh.

By the time we had finished cleaning the whole house and practiced our dance moves, we were very sweaty. The sweat smells under our arms filled the air with a musty scent of onions. Oh, we were pure-D musty fusty and giggly. The windows were raised and the doors were opened to expel the odor out of the house, and we could not stop laughing.

I loaned Lou money when she didn't have any. I scratched the dandruff out of her hair when no one else would. We were sisters and we were friends. She shared her friends to the point of them inviting me over to their homes to spend the night, and some of her friends had sisters my age who were students at the Lutheran Acad-emy School, which gave us lots to talk about. I enjoyed being with the sophisticated students of her class. Then the invitations stopped, and not even Lou visited her friends much. She stayed in the house or visited Randy, whom Mama thought she spent too much time with. That's why Mama wanted me to share the babysitting job with her. "To give her something to do," said Mama, "other than hang around that boy all the time."

Lou was one of those girls who kept a daily diary of her life. If she broke a fingernail, she wrote about it to "Dear Diary," and the diary was always locked, which only brought more suspicion to a young one like me. No one else seemed to care what was in that locked pink book except me. Each time I went into the chest of drawers to get clothing, I knew that the book was there, one drawer below mine, with her other belongings: slips, bras, sheers, and lots of other things that she didn't want to share or allow anyone to touch. I had never tried to open the lock on the diary, and I knew that if I did, she would know, so I stayed clear of her neatly packed drawer on the bottom, and anyway, I had enough on my mind to keep me thinking for a few days.

Finally, I was ready to make a plan. Late one afternoon I went to find Ben. His door was ajar, so I went directly inside, where he was napping on his bed. He had a way of stretching out his body that made him look longer than he was. He was almost seventeen years old and was not going to be a very tall man like Dah.

I watched him lying there on top of his bed, and although it was warm outside, a quilt was thrown over his feet. There was sunlight coming through the curtain over his window that cast a glow on his light brown skin.

Reddish tones appeared underneath the skin, which made his face glow like fading embers. His hair shone in three colors: light brown, dark brown, and golden brown around the edges of his face and temples. He had large brown hands with lovely clean square fingernails, and whispers of blond hair on his arms. His head was round and large. Ben was prone to hard red bumps breaking out on his face. He did his best to keep them clean, using Noxzema or alcohol to dry them up. So he was never short on Noxzema and alcohol.

Convinced that Ben was sound asleep, I took the liberty of looking around his room at all his things. There was a large bunch of change in a jar, with quarters and Indian head pennies. The Lincoln pennies and dimes with the ladies on them were many. Real silver dollars, keys, a knife, a watch and a chain, and some shoe polish, Juicy Fruit gum, and BBs.

Ben lay stretched out on a piece-worked quilt that sucked him down in a feathery mattress that Grandmama had given him for "being so kind" and taking her out to Hazen, Alabama, to church one Sunday. And she gave him the embroidered map of Kentucky that was hanging high behind his bed. I think she gave him a map of Kentucky because Dah laid a lot of crossties up there.

Dah had bought two guns for Ben from Sears, Roebuck: a BB gun and a pump shotgun, and their place was to stand attentively in a corner away from his bed, wrapped in flannel cases, unloaded. I picked up the small box where he kept his most special treasures he had found in the fields when we would be out helping with the weeding or harvesting. These were flints, arrowheads, and buttons from the Civil War, some with eagles on them, maybe from the uniforms of fallen soldiers who had long since disappeared. One by one I picked up the brass buttons and examined them, trying to read the embossed letters, which were flattened in places. Putting them back, I took up one of the half-dollars lying on the shelf.

"You could have that if you want. I got some more," he said, rubbing his eyes and stretching out. "What you doing in here anyway?" he asked, climbing out of the feather bed and resting his feet on the rug.

I answered, "I'm going to work tomorrow at Mrs. Nichols, so I won't be home till late. Then I'm off on Wednesday, and maybe that's when I will see that gal over there. Understand?" I asked.

He gave me a long look. "Yeah, I understand. Here's what you gon' do. Just act like you done forgot what happened, and tell her, if she brings it up, that you ain't mad and all's forgiven. She'll b'lieve you. Okay? Then start playing out in the yard, 'round the back, and not so close to them dogs. Best thing to do is take turns jumping rope or something. I'm going to drive up with the car and park on the sidewalk and come out where y'all at from the back door. Get her over here around about noontime, so I'll know and be ready. Don't worry about the rest of it. I know what to do."

Again I agreed with Ben. The plan was set and we were going to fix her real good. At least that's what I told myself, still trying to talk myself into it.

6.

The following day, Mrs. Nichols came a half hour earlier than usual because she needed help with the laundry. Cole was still living with her, so she had added wash to do. She drove me and the kids back to her home, and we picked up the laundry, which I helped her put in the back of the car. She had made a few sandwiches for the children to eat and also packed some of their favorite plastic toys to entertain them. Her hands overburdened with the extra items, she moved away from the trunk of the car to hand them to the kids through the car window. I noticed a new blue Dodge pickup sitting a few trailers away, with two white men in its cab. They were smoking and talking, with an occasional look in our direction. As we were about to drive off, their truck pulled out in front of us, then stopped. The men were dressed in dungaree work clothes and large cowboy hats. The driver apologized to Peggy, gave a wave, and then took off.

When we got to the laundromat, we both took the laundry bags inside and the children stayed outside in the car, playing. Mrs. Nichols put her laundry and Cole's into the washer, and I separated the children's clothes on the floor while she went into the back for coins.

Her son's laundry was soiled and stinking. It was going to take time to sort his clothes, between holding my breath and my nose and trying not to touch them with my hands, just with my fingertips. The smell was terrible, and I noticed the owner of the store, a red-faced white man in gray pants and a white short-sleeved shirt, walking my way. He seemed agitated about something. When he got close to me, he was mumbling, but I couldn't understand what he was saying. Maybe he was grumbling about the pee smell.

I kept my head down and continued sorting while Mrs. Nichols went to the car for the detergent and bleach and softener.

The owner was still mumbling at me, but I couldn't make out what he was saying. Then he came closer, and got right in my face, and said, "I have asked you to get out of my store, you nigger, and mor'n one time. Ain't gon' ask yer no mo'."

His face was flushed and angry to the point where his

lips were wet as if he was about to drool. His head had drops of sweat inside his thin hair and his brow was furrowed. He was now standing right over me.

Mrs. Nichols was fast approaching down the aisle, calling my name loudly. Her teased hair resembled a halo towering over her head, about to fall. Her eyes were wide. "Willie Mae! Willie Mae! Go! Head out to the car with the babies. I will finish up in here."

I felt my eyes watering up, but I refused to cry, even though I had heard him call me a nigger. No one had ever called me one to my face, and I couldn't understand why he had said it. I wasn't bad. I wasn't ugly or disrespectful. I was clean. These were not my clothes on the floor. I wanted to fight this old white man until he took his last breath.

I felt my fists balling up into knots as I heard Mrs. Nichols yell to me, "Go git in the car, Willie Mae! Please!"

I did as she asked. But I had a strong compelling desire to walk backward to the car, so that when I walked out of the laundromat's door, the wind would cleanse me and blow back on him his nasty disgusting ways and hateful energy, back into his doomed life. That's how I thought of him in that moment, as a doomed man, full of hate, bound for another hell even worse than the one he was living in.

My mind changed in an instant. I knew somehow that

I must not get mad. I stood outside the car door silently, facing the large windows of the store, and I could see Mrs. Nichols talking with the doomed white man. The anger was still inside me, and I pointed my finger at him through the windows and stared him down. My arm felt like lead when I put it at ease beside my body and returned to the car.

Suddenly I visualized Urmagene's face, maybe because she'd attacked me out of the blue as well.

One of the children asked, "How come you smiling, Willie Mae?" and I couldn't answer. Because, to me, I was still angry but not mad.

It was clear that Mrs. Nichols was upset as she got back into the car to drive us home. She drove fast and turned off into the gravel path to her house, the gravel picking up and hitting the back of the car. She slowed the car down to a stop and spoke to me through the rearview mirror.

"Willie Mae, there are some people in this world who are just mean. Mean enough to hurt anyone or anything living. That man is one of them, and had I known that, I would not have subjected you to it. I should have known better because of all that's happening in the newspapers and in Selma. I want you to start reading the papers more. I want you to forget about him. He is just that way. I'm so sorry. Now why don't y'all go into the house and watch some TV, and I will finish with the clothes." She kissed and hugged the kids and said bye-bye. I wanted to be kissed and hugged at that moment myself. I needed to be, so I walked up to her house with my arms around me, hugging myself.

Mrs. Nichols came back within a few hours, paid me, and took me home. She had canceled her plans for the rest of the day. Ben was there when I got home, his car in the yard. He was in the living room talking on the phone. Dah's car was gone and so was everyone else. Urmagene was sitting on the front porch of her house, and I beckoned for her to come to the fence and she came, looking greasy and stuffed.

"Yeah, you called me?" she asked, looking grown. "What you want?" She was shoeless and her feet were swollen in the patch of grass, looking like overcooked Vienna sausages in turnip greens.

I asked if she wanted to come over in a little bit to "jump rope and read some new funny papers."

She stood posing with one hand on her hip, popping gum. "Awh'ight," she said, accepting. "I'd be there directly." And she rolled away with her skirt hiked up in back, revealing rolls of fat in the folds of her knees.

I rushed into the house and told Ben to forget our plan for tomorrow because the fight was going to happen this afternoon. "Ben, just give me about fifteen minutes after she gets here to get her in the backyard. Go take care of the dogs!"

Ben looked surprised by my orders, holding his hand over the phone. "What you saying?" he asked me.

I yelled at him, "Get off the phone!"

Ben hung up the phone and asked me what was wrong.

I told him about the doomed man in the laundromat and asked him to find out where Mama and Dah were. Ben placed a call to Mrs. Beth's house in East Selma. When he got off the telephone, he told me that Mrs. Beth said that she and Mama were going over some things for the Eastern Stars meeting, and Dah had fallen asleep outside in the car. "Mrs. Beth told me that Mama had said not to wake up Dah on no count, 'less it's a 'mergency, and Mrs. Beth asked if we were okay, and I told her yes."

Ben now understood that I was ready to carry out our plan with Urmagene, so he put the dogs in the shed and gave them some water. He also raked up some of the dog mess and sprayed the area with the hosepipe. Mrs. Elnora and her family, our next-door neighbors to the other side, were away. Urmagene was taking her time to come over, so I washed my face and put Vaseline on it, and quickly changed into some blue jeans and tennis shoes. Ben took a seat close to the back door near the kitchen.

Urmagene rolled up in the yard slowly, still with the gum in her mouth. When she got up on the porch, she started looking through the comics I had placed in the swing, as if she was doing me a favor. She went through a few pages, and each one she pitched to the floor. "You ain't got nuthin new over here, and you told me you had some new stuff. I done seen ever' one of these," she said, still chewing and fast turning the pages. "Seen dat, seen dat, seen dat. What, what, what else you got?" she asked, looking away from me. Then she mumbled something under her breath.

"What did you say, Urmagene?" I asked.

"I said you wasted my time. I could be watching te-la-vision or something." She seemed frustrated.

"Urmagene, can I get you a cookie or some ice water? Maybe we could go in the backyard, and I'll turn the rope while you jump. What do you think?"

"Oh-kay," she said, getting up, pulling her stuck shorts out of her behind, as she followed me to the backyard.

I tied the rope to one side of the fence and started turning with the other end. I was waiting for Urmagene to jump smoothly in, but she didn't.

"No! No! No!" she cried out as she got hung up in the rope. "You can't even *turn*! Gimme dat rope so I can show you." She snatched the rope from me and we switched places.

Ben, having been listening inside, came out the back door and grabbed the rope from Urmagene's hands, and since we were so close, he pushed her up against me. She shoved me off her.

"HUNDEY, DON'T YOU LET HER PUSH YOU LIKE THAT!"

I started to cry, and Urmagene punched me on the shoulder with her fist. I punched her back in her face, and it didn't seem to hurt her because she was still chewing gum, and now she was coming at me so fast that I could tell this girl had fought before. She shoved me down. I looked for Ben, and his face was empty and focused on us. His mouth opened and he warned me not to look at him. "You better start fighting! Don't look at me, look at her!"

I was crying, dirt mixed with my tears, and I wanted to leave this meeting place. The girl was now sitting on my arm and punching me. Our dogs had begun to bark and struggle to get loose from the shed to rescue me. The dogs had sensed the danger and heard Ben's voice. He was screaming at me to "get up, roll over, get your ass up and beat her mean ass. If you let her whup you, you will deal with me later. Get up, Hundey."

I started jerking my body until she rolled off me, and I jumped on her and punched her in her side, the same side she had punched on me. I slapped her in the face a few times and told her to "turn your other goddamn cheek so the one I just slapped doesn't feel so bad. You hit me for no reason, Urmagene, and that's why I'm going to kick your ass."

I must admit, Urmagene almost got the best of me, but with Ben's coaching me and the threat of an ass-whipping from him if I got beaten, I had to make sure I won. I had to teach Urmagene not to ever hit me again. While she was on the ground, I grabbed a handful of her hair and pulled it hard. I told her to go tell her "Mammy" because I didn't care.

Then I jumped up off her and told Ben to turn the hose pipe on both of us and wash our legs down, so it looked like we were playing in the water and Urmagene was mad because she had gotten wet. "Now go tell your mama and watch her not believe your fast behind. Don't you ever hit me again or any of my family members, you crazy girl, and get out of this yard!"

Ben was soaking water all over us, and like lightning she ran home. Ben grabbed the yard rake to clean the backyard, and he let the dogs out and fed them. I went inside to clean up.

I felt so bad having ambushed her like that, but I felt like she deserved it. Soon Ben found me in my room, where I was crying. I don't even think it was the fight that was upsetting me. Ben sat down at the end of my bed and I told him about the doomed man at the laundromat, and he told me not to worry about it because that was what white crackers did anyway. He said all of them were the same. It was just that some of them didn't show it. He said he could deal better with the ones that showed their true selves than the ones who didn't. "Baby, no white man with a little bit of sense in his head at these times is gon' wait till you get up in his store and start washing clothes. He gon' stop you at the doe or he gonna go directly to the person who brought you in there in the first place. That woman you babysit for was wrong, and her ass needs to read more about what's going on here between races than SHE does. She should have asked that po-ass redneck before you got out of that car if you could come in. You know what," Ben said, lacing his shoes hastily and standing up from the bed, "Dah don't know about this mess yet, 'cause if he did . . . your mama in trouble."

I jumped up, hot! "What you mean, 'your mama'! She is your mama, too, Maine! You crazy?" I asked him.

"Now don't you jump your ass up at me, little girl," he said, pushing my shoulders down. "She gon' be in trouble and I ain't going to do nothing about it. Mama shouldn't have let you go work a day for that woman. We are marching here in Selma, protesting, rallying, and people are being beaten and getting kilt out there, maybe as we talk."

I got up and grabbed the towel I had been using to get the water out of my head, and walked out of the room. Ben was still yelling. "We got a war going on, a civil war, and everybody's messed up. Ain't no telling what could happen to us or you over there with her. You don't need no money."

7.

Later that afternoon somebody was coming up on the porch as I started down the hall. It was Joe peering through the screen door, head and neck stretching to see if he could see anybody. He seemed anxious.

"Hey der, Wil' Mae." He cut off my name and asked me if my dad was home, and I told him no and that Ben and I were on our way out to East Selma to get Dah and Mama. Joe wanted to see Ben. I called for Ben to come to the door, and Joe asked Ben if he had been here when Urmagene came over to play. Ben said yes, he had, and asked what was the matter.

"Just ask your daddy to come by and see me fo' he turn in tonight, please," Joe replied.

"Yes, sir, I sure will," said Ben.

Joe walked off the porch toward his house. He seemed to be upset about something, and I knew what it was, but I couldn't care at that moment. Ben decided to go out to East Selma to see Dah and Mama. He wanted to get to Dah before Joe did. "Now, Willie Mae, you just stay home with the doors locked and let me take care of this."

An hour later, Ben was back. He told me that he and Dah had spoken at length about everything that happened with Urmagene and me, and how Urmagene started it all. "I witnessed the whole thing," Ben had said.

Dah had assured Ben that he would talk to Joe when he got home, no matter what time it was. Dah told Ben, "They are nice people and they pay their bills on time. I don't want any foolishness going on to cause them to leave." He wanted someone like Joe in the rental house because of the talks of boycotts and more marches. He said that Joe was a no-nonsense man and he came from a good family of people in York, Alabama.

Ben told me that Dah had said that Joe's daddy was the son of a sharecropper who eventually owned acres of land over in York, near Mississippi. "Still do," Ben added. "Bertha and Joe met and was married less than a year when she come up with that girl they got. That's not Joe's first child. He got another one, a boy about fifteen or sixteen, in Mobile, with the child's mama and the man the child's mama married after she and Joe broke up. Serinna, that's her name. She's a nurse and don't look anything like Bertha. Both of them are like night and day. One light-skinned and small, the other dark and heavy. Mama says Bertha was the only one took pity on

Joe when the divorce come through. Before the divorce, folks claim Joe drove around with Serinna like he had a 'Ejypshun queen' on his side. Everywhere you saw her, you saw him."

Ben cautioned me, "Willie Mae, Dah had been drinking when he told me this, so he was open to talking. Just don't mention what you and I talked about tonight."

I agreed, crossed my heart and hoped to die if I did.

When he and Mama got back to the house from East Selma, Dah called Joe over and they had a talk on the porch. While my sisters slept hard in our room, I could hear the conversation through the open window.

"Now, Joe, don't you let them chillren come between you and me! Hear me. Let them work it out, 'cause we weren't there and hit ain't no sense in gitting 'volved in it. Now, I know Maine, and he gon' take up for his susta, but he ain't gon' let her go too fa', b'lieve me on dat! You know what I mean?" he asked Joe.

Joe agreed to let it go, and Dah came home and went to bed after telling Mama to straighten us out some kind a way, because we might be getting too grown and smelling our tails.

The next day, Mama screamed at me and Ben. She told me that she should slap both of us on our behinds, which made us quiet for a few days, and we stayed out of her way.

We saw plenty of Urmagene after that. She would

come over to visit us, look through comic books, and swing in our swing. She and I never had an easy friendship, though, and I wasn't unhappy when, after only a little while, she and her parents moved on.

During the six months of her family's stay, Dah said they had prospered nicely working and saving their money. Bertha was grateful as always and spoke to Dah about moving to Bessemer, Alabama, where she could possibly get work in one of the school cafeterias. Dah encouraged her to visit Bessemer first and drive around the town and countryside. Dah had been to Birmingham many times, and the two cities were close. He said that Joe could possibly have a chance to work in one of the factories where they produced goods from steel, and the chance of Bertha opening her own business was promising. Mama thought this was all good news and she spoke about how much she enjoyed the town when she was there. Mama saw the light in Bertha's eyes, the same light she saw when Bertha was moving into our rental house, and she knew they would be happy there.

Dah Finds Out

Trouble seemed to follow me that summer. I went back to work for Mrs. Nichols one Friday afternoon after she called with an emergency. Fridays were usually her day off, but one of the waitresses at the bar hadn't come in for work because her baby was sick and she couldn't get a sitter, so the job called Mrs. Nichols to fill in. Mama told her that I could do it only if I could be home before dark and that this would possibly be the last week of work for me and she hoped Mrs. Nichols understood. She did, and would start her search for a permanent sitter before school started. Also, Cole was finishing his project and leaving town soon.

That afternoon her kids and I watched TV and played in the trailer all day, stopping only to eat dinner. The children asked for hot dogs. I boiled the wieners in a pot on the stove. Before the next show came on the TV, I helped the girl with her bath. Her brother fell asleep on the floor that evening, and I put him to bed during a commercial so as not to miss the movie I was watching with his sister, who fell asleep shortly after dinner.

Around seven thirty that evening, a car pulled up into the driveway. I thought it was Mrs. Nichols and went to the window to check. It was not her car and not Cole's. Two white men were inside. I thought maybe they was making a U-turn in the driveway to go back out to the main road. I picked up the little girl and put her in bed. When I came back out of her room the car was still sitting in the driveway, but the driver was not in the car. The passenger, a male, was alone in the vehicle. Now I recognized the car from a few days earlier, pulling out in front of us that one time.

Suddenly there was a knock on the front door of the trailer, and a man's voice said that he wanted to leave a message for Mrs. Nichols. I put the chain in place and told him through the closed door that she was not home, and he asked me if she was working. I replied that he could go to the bar to see her, but he wanted to come in to leave a note.

My pulse pounding, I asked him to wait a moment. I quietly made sure the dead bolt was locked. I did not feel good about this man, and even though I could not view him clearly through the frosted glass in the door, I felt that I had seen him somewhere before. I walked quickly to the back door and saw a figure approaching the back of the trailer. It was probably the passenger in the car. I got to the door quickly and checked it, too. Its chain and lock were secure.

In a panic now, I picked up the telephone and called the bar. Someone went to get Mrs. Nichols as I heard the man out front knocking harder on the door. Stretching the phone's long cord, I peeped out a back window. The second man was somewhere out there but I couldn't see him, yet I could smell his cigarette through a back window that was cracked open. The tiny window wasn't hardly big enough to get a hand through, but I rushed to close and lock it tightly.

Just as Mrs. Nichols came to the telephone, the car outside started up, but it didn't seem to be driving away. Maneuvering to the front, I caught a glimpse of the driver's face and it was one of the men who had been sitting near her house in a blue truck the day I helped her with the laundry. Then I glimpsed the passenger. It was both of the men. They were up to no good. I knew that they had been trying to get inside the house. I told her what was happening and that I was going to call my father to come for me.

Then it happened. There was a loud *BOOM!* from underneath the house.

The men were trying to scare me out of the house. I could hear water starting to pour from underneath the trailer. Whatever had exploded had cracked a water pipe. Somehow, the kids didn't wake up.

"Mrs. Nichols!" I screamed. "These men are trying to get in here!" I told her about the explosion.

I could hear her but her voice was muffled. She was talking to someone. It was Cole. He was at the bar with her and would rush home to check on us.

"Don't answer the door, Willie Mae," she begged me. "I'm going to stay on the phone until he gets there."

"Should I call the police?" I asked.

Mrs. Nichols hesitated. "No," she said. "Probably not."

I was so scared. I stretched the long cord on the phone across the kitchen so I could reach into the utensil drawer. I found a knife and an ice pick. I sat on the floor halfway between the two doors. The children were still asleep. Things were happening so fast. Then I heard car doors slam and tires spinning in the gravel driveway. Then a racing engine and more skidding tires.

A few minutes later, someone at the door said, "Open the door, Willie Mae. It's me, Cole." I was so scared that he had to shout and knock a few times before I got up off the floor. I was still on the phone with Mrs. Nichols.

"Willie Mae, did Cole get there yet?" she asked me.

I told her that he had, and that the men had left. I got up and let Cole in.

Cole said he was going to put the kids in the car and

take me home. I was too stunned and didn't acknowledge him. Then he noticed the sound of the broken pipe under the trailer and went outside to investigate. Eventually the water stopped. Cole came back inside and said he had shut the water off at the main and would repair it tomorrow.

"Willie Mae, I promise you I will find out the reason behind all this." He told me that one of the men had broken the water pipe on purpose with a powerful firecracker and that I was right to remain in the house, because who knew what their intentions were. He told me that he and Mrs. Nichols would speak with my parents about the incident.

I spoke up and told Cole that I was going to tell my daddy as soon as I got in the house and that he better get to Dah before I did, and I wondered how he was going to do that because I was riding in the back seat and he was driving.

Cole's car pulled up on the sidewalk outside our house and I noticed another car in the driveway. It was Mrs. Nichols's convertible. She had gone ahead of Cole and was waiting for us on the front porch. She was talking to Mama alone. Dah's and Ben's cars were not on the property.

I jumped out of the car as soon as it stopped. I ran up on the porch and stood close to Mama. Cole stayed behind the wheel of the car with the children in the back seat.

"You all right, Hundey?" Mama asked.

"Yes, ma'am," I answered.

"Did those men touch you at all?" she asked, looking at me closely.

"No'm, they didn't. They scared me and tried to break into her house, Mama, and I had seen them around her neighborhood once before when I first started over there. They were sitting in a truck, and they cut out in front of her car as we pulled out."

Mrs. Nichols was staring at Mama as I spoke, and she looked worried and tired. She appeared to tremble inside herself. She was shaking hard, as if she was going to have a conniption fit.

Mama's face was changed. No longer did she present the welcoming smile she wore with any person she met. No longer was her face smooth. Now she wore the face as if she was smelling something, something ugly. Now things were hitting home, and on our porch was this white woman, telling Mama things that had jeopardized the life of her daughter, her baby. Mama had gone against Dah's wishes, and now something had interrupted the innocence of one of her own children.

I could almost hear Mama thinking and knew that she

was hot. I knew that she wasn't thinking about the anger that Dah would have collecting in him once she told him what had happened. Her thoughts were on those men and why they had come after us children. She knew Mrs. Nichols felt sorry, but did this woman know these men? Were they there to collect something from her? Mama waved a floating column of gnats out of her face as Mrs. Nichols spoke about her regrets.

"That's fine, Mrs. Nichols," said Mama in a clear, calm, and even voice. "I 'preciate your words, but my husband gon' take this matter upon himself, and I assure you everything will work itself out. If you don't know them, and you said that you didn't, then I have no other reason to not take your word for it. Now, I am not my husband, and I won't speak for him. But there's lots going on here in Selma with people killing coloreds and coloreds going missing, and downtown there, people are divided by a clothesline, one that the sheriff has strung across Sylvan Street to keep us from protesting. That just shows us that some people will do anything to satisfy their greed, anger, and stupidity against one another."

"Well now, Katie," Mrs. Nichols said. "I don't think this was anything to do with all that business. Those men were probably just harmless burglars who got scared off when they found out someone was home."

That tripped a switch inside Mama. Her anger exploded.

"Harmless burglars? I don't hear too much about burglars. But you seem to want me to think that this was probably what they were trying to do," Mama said. "And what I believe is that those men were after you in some fashion. And that the opportunity came about that Hundey was there alone with your young'uns. Those men were going to hurt your chillren and my daughter because of something YOU had done. And this IS a form of robbery—to rob children of their innocence with this. Yes . . . you are right in your thinking of a robbery."

As I listened, I thought about the day weeks earlier when I'd first seen those men, and how Mrs. Nichols had seen them also but ignored them, maybe because she did not want me to witness anything between her and them.

Being the God-fearing and nonjudgmental person that she was, Mama shocked me by the last words she said to Mrs. Nichols. "I don't care at this moment if you as a white woman feel that I am disrespecting you in any way. I want to assure you that I have no respect for what you have put these children through. I don't care about the times we are living in at this moment because at this moment I take a stand. You are spinning a story, not telling me the truth, and that's why you got here before that man o' yours did. You didn't want him hearing these lies that are coming out of your mouth. If you lie, you will steal, and that man Cole ain't yours, and you know what I'm talking about. I told you just this morning that today was my daughter's last day because I felt something wasn't right, and now look at this here. You got children, too. Think about that. Now you go on out there to your car, and take your babies home, and be thankful that *my* daughter had the good God-given sense to protect them and herself. And, Mrs. Nichols, be thankful my daughter is physically untouched, be very thankful." Mama said all of this, looking Mrs. Nichols in the eye.

Mama didn't cry, and I felt so proud of her. She took me by the hand and brought me inside the house, putting the hook in the eye latch on the screen door, leaving the woman to stagger off the front porch alone.

When she told Dah all about my job with Mrs. Nichols and what had happened, he didn't argue with Mama and he didn't hold it against her, but he did tell her to keep us in the house for a few days, no running back and forth to the store or sitting on the porch by ourselves. He said that he was going down in the country with some of his friends, and they were going game hunting and taking Ben with them. He had asked Joe next door to look out for us at the house. Dah also said that Cole was leaving Selma in a few days, later than he had expected to, due to what had happened at the trailer.

"Cole ain't nothing to play with, Kate, and I know that 'cause I talked with him, and he rest-assured me and my boy that he was gon' git to the bottom of it. And, Kate, I feel sorry for the person when he and his boys get hold of them. I am just . . . I don't want no trouble right now. Let him take care of it. That's a close call on them and us. If I had to go looking for them two men, it would've been hard on them. Cole owes me. I've called him out on it, and he heard me."

Dah removed his hat and ran the white handkerchief over his head and face. He spoke as if in prayer:

White man the biggest enemy ever.
Low-down.
Lord have mercy.

Puppy

One Sunday morning we all were late for church. Dah was complaining that Mama had kept him up too late and he had overslept. Mama blamed him, and all of us children blamed each other. We all got dressed quickly, happy to be going to the country. The girls made slick ponytails in their hair, and each one helped the other dress up.

Dah got us all in the car and called to our dog Puppy, a dark brown cocker spaniel, "Puppy, come on, girl, get from under there and come get your breakfast."

The dog didn't come, so Dah reached down and drew her from underneath the car, and sat her in front of her bowl near the driveway.

Mama came out but had to go back inside to get something she had forgotten.

"Hurry up, Kate, we red' to go," called Dah.

"Okay, honey, I will. Go 'head and pull out!" she yelled back.

Dah started the car and begin to drive backward when

we all heard a loud yelp. It was Puppy! She had left her bowl and crawled back under the car to continue sleeping. Everyone screamed. Dah cursed hard and loud. He jumped from the car, walking fast around the side as we held our breath and ears, listening to Puppy's low moans.

"Pup-paay! Aw, Lard! Come here, girl, come on," he said, begging for her to get up.

And then we knew. We knew when the other dogs, the hounds, began to howl. Something was very wrong with Puppy.

Dah couldn't reach Puppy. He jumped into the car and gently moved it so that he could get to her. Then he jumped out of the car and saw that she was still breathing, but bloody. By now Dah had begun to stomp his foot on the ground and pound his fist into his hand, cussing. He was helpless, knowing that he couldn't save the puppy and seeing Mama standing near the car with us, watching him struggle.

He lashed out at us: "Y'all git in the house!"

Then he lowered his heavy head and raised an apology in the tone of his voice. "Kate, please, honey. Take them chillren in the house! I'll be right back."

Mama had water in her eyes when she opened the car door on the other side to usher us all back into the house. I ran to the window against Mama's will and saw Dah pick up Puppy and take her to the junk house, where he kept his tools. When he came back into the house, Dah changed his clothes and stated that we were all going to miss Sunday school, but we were still going to church. Mama needed a few minutes to find a blanket to wrap Puppy in.

While she was looking, Maine went out to turn on the hose pipe and clean the grass where Puppy had been hit. Then we were ready to leave.

When it was time to go, Dah went back to the junk house with the blanket, and then appeared carrying her wrapped body, which he carefully loaded into the back of the car. He went back to fetch a shovel and then it was time to drive to Orrville. No one said anything in the car for at least a mile. We all just cried softly with our heads bowed low.

Thinking about Puppy, the spots of her blood in the dirt, made me wonder how awful Dah felt about running the car over her. I softly prayed through my tears. *Oh dear God, please forgive Dah. He didn't mean it. We were coming to your church when this happened. Dah loved Puppy and so did I. Jesus, we never knew where Puppy came from, she just was there one day. She was so pretty and brown. Dah loves the color brown. We just wanted to take care of her. She was quiet and soft. We tried to take good care of her and now she's gone. I am so sorry we hurt her. Please protect her when you get to see her. Amen.*

Mama never turned around to look at us the whole

ride. The only thing we could see was the back of her head and the veil of lace jutting from her church hat. Dah kept his hands tightly gripped on the steering wheel.

Then Mama spoke to us: "There will be no more dogs 'cept the hunting dogs. No more pets, y'all. What has happened here was an accident and shouldn't be spoken about in church. We will bury Puppy out here in Orrville with our family members, and that is that," she said, softly wiping her eyes with her handkerchief.

And that was how it was after that. No more pets. Just Dah's two hunting dogs. One was Nina, a black hound that could track and find anyone at any time. Nina was the best hunting dog in Selma, yet her identical twin, Gurl, was quite the opposite. She was fast on her feet and loved to give chase but was unable to follow a scent.

"Wake up, Brown!" the lawman's voice called in the middle of the night, and a hard banging erupted on Dah's side of the house, startling us all from sleep. "Come on, Brown, get up now."

"Who's that out there?" Dah asked from his bed as we all listened.

I jumped out of bed and peeked out the door of our bedroom and saw Mama standing in Dah's doorway.

"It's me, Brown, Buster Shell and Walter Tom! We got

a colored boy that's broke out and's running like a jack-rabbit."

"So what he done and why y'all out here in town? Why don't y'all call on Clay? He got dogs."

"Come on, Brown! Now you know you've got better hounds 'n anybody's! That boy broke in a house over there by the ballpark and they ast me to go git him and that's what I'm gon' do!"

The man cleared his throat of phlegm and repeated himself: "That's what I'm gon' do."

Dah lay still for a minute, thinking, coughing, whispering to Mama. "I don't feel like this tonight, Kate. That's two of the sheriff's boys out there. They want them dogs o' mine. What time my watch got over there, ba'y?"

"Two."

Dah swore.

"Ask 'em who it is they looking for," whispered Mama.

Dah propped himself up on his elbows in bed, his long neck straining toward the curtained window. The skin around his Adam's apple tightened, and its sharp trigger jerked upward, then lowered itself after each spoken word. "Mr. Shell!" he yelled as the dogs barked at the sound of Dah's voice. He called out again, "Mr. Shell!"

One of the men answered.

"Who you got running, boss?" Dah asked, trying not to sound too interested.

A voice returned an answer. "Ol' Duke's boy! Brown, you don't have to come, yo' dogs know me. You can loan 'em to me, ain't nuthing gon' happen to 'em."

I could hear Mama as she whispered in a quivering voice, "Oh no! No! That boy is a good boy. What's goin' on, Brown? They got the wrong one. I know who they looking for, and he been gone since yestdiddy."

"Don't worry, susta, I know what to do," Dah said, reassuring her. The iron springs creaked with the sound of him crossing over the side of the bed to yell out the window, "I don't loan my dogs to nobody. Just hold on. I'll be out there directly."

"Brown, be careful, please!" Mama warned, softly gripping Dah's wrist with her hand.

"Kate, go check them girls befo' I go. Come on now," Dah said as he started to get dressed. "I'll talk to Maine before I go."

I hurried back to bed and lay awake, listening, until I heard Mama open our bedroom door and look in. She saw us girls all pretending to be asleep and closed the door.

All four of us girls got up and went to the window. We could see the front porch and Dah's side of the house. I saw three men standing outside near Dah's bedroom window, carrying flashlights and shotguns. In the glare of their flashlights, I could see their red faces and recognized

Mr. Tom and Mr. Shell. They were looking at our dogs, Nina and her twin, chained to a post under the house. Next to Mr. Tom stood another white man with a lump of tobacco in his jaw, chewing as he released the brown liquid onto the ground with a hard spit.

The dogs came up from under the house as far as their chains would allow and approached the men, sniffing at the ground where the spit congealed. Mr. Shell produced a worn tenny shoe and held it under each dog's nose. On his side of the house, Dah stepped out a side door we never used, closed the door behind him, and stepped into the ring of men, eyeing them evenly. Dah was dressed in his hunting clothes and greeted the men with a nod of his head. They exchanged words that I could not hear.

Dah disappeared into the house again, telling Mama that he forgot something. When he returned to the group, he was carrying his pistol and a carbine. The men returned to their car, parked on Second Avenue. Dah unchained the dogs and brought them around front, where he put them in the back of his station wagon and shut the door. He then got in and turned on the ignition.

After backing out of the driveway, letting the men lead, Dah followed with the dogs.

Mama locked the doors to the house, and we all went back to bed and lay awake until the morning sun broke through the night sky.

The house was stiff with quietness until I finally heard Dah's car return. Soon came the rattle of the chains as he secured the hounds in their kennel under the house. Relieved, I knew that Dah and the animals were all right.

My sisters and I got up and went to the window, where we saw Dah giving them bowls of water. Both of them were filthy.

"Good dogs," Dah said, patting them down and rubbing their backs. He fed them. "Good dogs!"

When Dah finally stepped into the house, I could hear the murmur of their conversation and then Mama say, "Thank you, Jesus. How much farther does he have to go?"

"Ferguson swamp and he's clear. He'll make it, and he knows the way from there. When he done some work for me in the past, I took him and Maine all through that swamp and showed them how to move through it. He gon' make it."

Hearing this, I knew Mama would feel some relief, because every son was her son and her heart prayed for them all.

An Unfriendly Visitor

Selma was a quiet place to live. There was no traffic in the streets or cars honking or children staying out late at night, making a ruckus up and down the sidewalks. The only noise you occasionally heard was the siren of a police car or an ambulance, and you could pretty much set your watch by the passing trains and their lonely whistles. If you heard loud voices in the street late at night, like eight or nine o'clock, you could bet that someone somewhere recognized the voice, and the person was confronted with a friendly complaint the next time he or she was seen.

Like the time Terry Lee and Mary Huntly were arguing over a box of Cracker Jack on their way home from Deak D'Ampars's store.

The next day Mama saw Mary walk by while I was helping her with potting her begonias on the front porch. She stood up and called out to the young teenager.

"Mary, I know I heard you last evening out chere with Terry, fussing over a ten-cent box of them ol' sweet Cracker Jacks. You know better'n to be so loud at night, when folks trying to sleep. Who taught you that?" she asked.

"Oh! No'm, Mrs. Brown, you see it wasn't like dat. Terlee always picking on me," she said, grinning. "I didn't mean no harm—I'm sawry, Mrs. Brown. It ain't gon' happen no mo'. Thank you for telling me. I'm gon' tell Terlee you mad at both of us. He won't like that 'cause he love him some Mrs. Brown. And watch him come running over here to 'pologize. Mrs. Brown, I don't know if you know this, but Terlee is a straight-A student, and he don't git out much, so when he does, he go kinna crazy," she said with a broad smile.

"Mary, I ain't mad at neither one y'all," Mama said. "I just know your mama real good, and you and Terry Lee going to be somebody one day. And I never heard you loud like that. Don't do that no more out here in the streets. You a girl. Girls ain't loud." Mama blew her a kiss and went back to her potting. "Say hello to Augustine for me, please."

"Okay, Mrs. Brown. No hard feelings."

"None taken, Mary."

Mama threw up the back of her hand with an airy wave

and kept working. She wasn't going to tell on Mary. She just wanted to warn her that someone was watching.

In Selma, someone was always watching.

Watching the Negroes,

watching the whites,

watching the whites watch the Negroes,

watching the neighbors,

watching out for the neighbors,

watching out for the sick,

watching out for the old, the new, the needy, the crooks, the wayward youngsters.

Selma was small, and a small town always has a watchful eye.

Weren't nobody watching me and Chauncey in the hallway that Saturday afternoon, however. Mama and Dah had gone to the grocery store, leaving me in charge. This was in our new house, a couple years before the incident at Mrs. Nichols's trailer. We were playing jacks, and the hard oak floor was the perfect surface.

Chauncey couldn't play as well as me because her hands were smaller and she was desperate to beat me. She was all right with onesies and twosies, but when it came to the higher numbers, she sometimes needed several tries to pick up the right number of jacks before catching the ball on one bounce. I told her it was okay that she did it this way, 'cause you can't always go by the instructions.

By us doing it our way, she won all the games, and I was happy to let her keep on playing till she wanted to stop. We must have been on that hard oak floor for an hour or more when I noticed that she had gotten the hang of the game and was really winning, and I told her so, which made her smile.

"Chauncey, you are playing really good," I said. "Look at you. Shoot! Okay, let me get a game now. You've been playing for a while."

She didn't pay me no mind. She just pushed my hand out the way and kept throwing the ball and scraping up the jacks.

"Come on, now, let me have the ball," I said.

Chauncey was up on her knees and playing with all her might. Both of us had our heads down, focused on the game, when I heard a car door slam out front. I turned to look out the screen door. I saw Mr. Ray's car, a mint-green Cadillac, sitting on the sidewalk in front of the house. Mr. Ray was sitting behind the wheel, and a man whom I recognized was walking up on the front porch. It was Mr. Tate. I could tell from his bushy head of hair.

He came up on the porch, staggering a bit, the print of a pint in his front pants pocket.

Now, being that I was the oldest one home, I got up to greet him. I put the hook on the door and spoke to him through the screen. "Hi, Mr. Tate."

"Hey there. Is your daddy home?" he asked.

"No, sir, he ain't. They ain't here. Everyone went out to the grocery store," I said.

"Well, he asked me to stop by and pick up some cans of paint. Did he leave anything lack that here for me?" he asked.

"No, sir," I answered.

"Well," he said, looking away from me like he was thinking hard. "Okay. Where is your brother Ben? Maybe he knows where Brown left them cans." He still didn't look at me.

"He ain't here, either," I said.

"So ain't nobody here but you and her?"

"Yes, sir," I answered softly. "We here by ourselves. But we ain't doing nothing wrong. We just playing."

"What y'all playing?" he asked.

"Jacks," I answered.

"Y'all playing jacks? Well, that's good." Then he reached for the handle on the screen door, and I told him that it was locked.

He said, "That's good. But you know me, right?"

I said, "Yes, sir."

Chauncey was still playing, but off her knees and

sitting on the floor now. Mr. Tate said, "You see this change here?" as he went into his pocket and pulled out a handful of coins. "Well, I am going to give y'all all of it if you let me come in and play with you." He jerked at the door and the hook jumped out.

Mr. Tate had given us money before, but Mama or Dah was always around, and he would ask them if it was okay. Usually it was Mama who gave the okay.

I was startled and jumped back. He opened the door slightly and stuck his loaded hand inside. I was confused, but I took the money from his open palm.

He laughed as if we were playing a game, but it didn't feel right.

I yelled for Chauncey to "Run fast! Run out the back door!"

She shrieked and flew out back with me right behind her, and I yelled to Mr. Tate, "I'm going to tell my daddy you were here."

I don't think he heard me because Chauncey was screaming so loud.

We got out back and I calmed her down. She was shaking, and tears were dripping down to her chin. "What they want, Hundey? What they want?" she kept saying.

The dogs in their pen were barking, startled out of their naps by the commotion.

"Nothing, nothing," I said, putting my arms around her.

I heard the car door slam and then Mr. Ray's car drove off fast with a squeal of the tires.

I turned on the spigot in the yard and washed Chauncey's face with the water and my hand, which felt dirty.

We were both shaking as we walked around the house to the front porch. I set Chauncey down in the swing and went tiptoeing inside to check the house.

No one was there. It seemed like an eternity just walking around in my own home, looking in each room, making sure we were safe. Then I went back on the porch with my sister, who had worried herself to sleep in the swing. I thought it would be best to pick her up and put her across the bed in our room. I took a nap with her.

An hour later, Dah and Mama drove up to the house.

I could tell from their voices that Mama was not in a good mood. Usually she wasn't when they went shopping together, because Dah would leave her to pay for all the food. If she complained that he was taking all her money, he would remind her: "Kate, I come home every time I get paid and give you everything 'cept what I need to get by on for the week." But Mama might start pouting and talking under her breath till she was mad enough to ride all the way home from Gaston's IGA supermarket downtown in the back seat of the car.

I was groggy from sleep, so the incident earlier slipped my memory until I heard Dah's voice and the jingle of coins in my skirt pocket.

I was scared to tell Dah what had happened, scared that I had overreacted and done something wrong, but I felt that I had to tell Dah that Mr. Tate had come by with Mr. Ray because Mr. Ray was there to see Dah.

So I went on the porch to tell them of his visit, and Dah asked me, "What did he say he wanted?"

I told him, "He came here for some paint that you promised him."

And Dah replied, "Yeah, I know. Now help take this groc'y in the house, you and Chauncey." He went back to bring more bags from the car.

I noticed how nicely both of them were dressed. Dah wore a soft brown pigskin jacket and white shirt and gray trousers. Mama had on a sheer green belted dress with a white slip underneath that showed off the dress's print of leaves, and she wore a low-heeled black pair of shoes.

"What you standing there for, Hundey?" Mama snapped, taking out her frustration at Dah on me. "Stop lookin' at dem bags and take 'em in the house."

As he carried up the last bags from the car, Dah looked at me and smiled. I reached down to pick up a bag and again heard the jingle of the change in my skirt pocket.

"Dah, Mr. Tate gave me and Chauncey this money," I

said, snatching up the coins and stretching out my hand to him. "He said he wanted to come in and play with us and that we could have the money if I let him in."

Dah's smile vanished.

I kept talking. "I didn't let him in. He pulled on the door and the hook came off, so he reached in and I grabbed at the money and then I grabbed Chauncey and ran out the back door. Dah, we didn't do nothing wrong," I said.

Dah stood silently with his hands on his hips and his head down, his back toward Mama.

Mama said to me, "Hundey, girl, did you say anythang to make him want to come up in this house?"

"Do what? I didn't do anything, Mama," I pleaded. "I promise."

Mama called out his name loudly, "Brown!"

Dah wouldn't answer.

"Brown! Brown! What you thankin'?" she yelled, trying to break his trance.

Dah didn't answer.

I offered the money to him. "Here, Dah, this is the money he gave me," I said, stretching out my hands.

"I don't want it," Dah said, looking strangely sad and distant.

Mama's eyes were wild and bulging as Dah started walking to his car.

Halfway there, he stopped and turned to me. "Hundey, take the rest of those bags in the house and close the front door, and, Kate, you go on in there with them."

Mama wasn't having it. "I'm not going nowhere in no house, and where you goin', Brown?"

He didn't answer her and she turned her wild look on me, pointing a red polished arrowhead-shaped fingernail at my face. "Gal, I hope you didn't say anything to that man. Your daddy 'bout to—" and she stopped herself.

"What makes you think she did something to him?" Daddy hollered. Pointing to me, he said, "These chere my babies, Kate! That man came up here on *my* front porch." Dah didn't flinch. "You takin' up for him, Kate?"

"I ain't taking up for him, Brown," said Mama. She lowered her voice. "I just want to . . . I just want to get to the bottom of this before things get bad."

"Thangs got bad when that man pulled the handle of my do'. You don't 'cuse my baby 'bout something she don't know nothing about. She tried to throw him off. She did the best she could. So you don't get to the bottom of nothing! I'm going to do that," he said, looking her in the face. "I'm going to get Tate. That's where I am going. I want to talk to him."

Mama's eyes were like saucers, and she was scared. "Lord!" she said, trembling, and Dah turn around and walked to the car. As he did, Mama ran and jumped into the back seat before Dah could stop her, and slowly they drove off toward East Selma.

Mr. Ray owned a candy store out in East Selma, close to one of Dah's good friends, Mr. Dan. Mr. Ray employed a woman named Jet, whom he trusted behind the cash register and to fry and serve fish sandwiches at his store on Friday and Saturday nights, which brought in more customers. Mr. Ray and Mr. Tate were known to ride around sometimes on Fridays and Saturdays, and, at some point, would surely be in East Selma before the store got too crowded for Jet to handle. So Dah and Mama went to visit their friends Mr. Dan and his wife, who lived in close proximity to Mr. Ray's store, and gave Mr. Ray time to drive around and relax.

I guess because I was so young it didn't occur to me just how bad things could get. So I went along with my day and my sister Chauncey, playing and watching television. By seven thirty that evening, Mama and Dah had not come home, but my sisters and I were in the house: me, Chauncey, Noonchi, and Lou. Maine was sure to be in East Selma, because he had just started courting Evelyn, Mildred White's daughter.

Noonchi and Lou wanted to know where our parents were. I told them what had happened, and Noonchi got on the phone right away and called out to Evelyn's house to see if Maine was there. He was, and when she got him on the phone, I heard her ask, "Listen, Maine, have you seen Dah?"

And I guess his answer was no because she yelled at him, "Walk right over to Mr. Dan's house to see if everything is okay, and call back to let me know."

I could see the fear in her eyes, and then I got real scared.

Noonchi gave me a hug and then talked serious to me. "Hundey, Mr. Tate is a grown man and was supposed to be Dah's friend. But it sounds like he wanted to harm you and Chauncey, and he should know better. He is in a lot of trouble. If Dah goes to the police, they could lock him up in jail. I am not sure, but with all the hatred for colored people going on here, you don't know what they might do."

Noonchi held my hand and said that I had done the right thing by running out of the house. Lou said that she thought I should have gone to Mama in private to keep it away from Dah. "Dah is a very serious man, Hundey. You have to be careful about what you let him know, because he can be hard to deal with. Don't worry. Maine is going to find out if anything happened. You and Chauncey go take a bath, and we will wait for the call."

The call never came, but Mama, Dah, and Ben came home after nine that night. I remember both cars pulling up in the driveway and Dah going straight to his room, returning shortly to sit in his favorite spot on the porch. Maine sat out there next to him. Mama came in boiling mad. She flew into the dining room where I was sitting, looking wild and hot. "Your daddy almost killed a man tonight. You hear me, girls! And we still don't know if he's going to make it." She had big, hot tears rolling out of her eyes and a sweating forehead. She went back to Dah's room and closed the door.

I didn't know how to feel. I felt like I was wrong for reporting something to my daddy that I knew I was right to tell him. I didn't know that Dah was going to nearly kill a man. I felt so alone because no one was explaining to me what had happened.

Then Dah came in and went into his room. I could hear murmuring voices through the closed door. When Dah reappeared, he went back out to the porch. Maine stayed near him all night. Mama's door stayed closed. Our house went dark, and I was lonely again, so I climbed in bed with Chauncey and fell asleep crying.

Sometimes a good sleep and a good cry is all that's needed. Once I found my way out of the white bedsheet I had rolled up in during the night, I was able to breathe and smell the sage sausage cooking in the kitchen. It was after seven in the morning and everybody was in the kitchen, eating. When I came in, I saw there were also two other men in our house with Dah: Mr. Ray and a man I didn't know by face. They were sitting at the table, having a friendly conversation and drinking freshly percolated coffee, out of teacups, which Mama used for comp'ny. The man was Buddy, Tate's stepbrother.

"Buddy," said Dah, "I do appreciate y'all coming by here and telling me this news, and this ain't going no further."

"And, Mr. and Mrs. Brown," said Buddy, "I'm truly sorry for what my brother did. Girls, you have my apologies, too. I been knowing y'all a long time and like I told Jim, I said, 'Jim, you got to stop with the drinking 'fore you hurt somebody or somebody hurt you.' And now look at this mess. He lucky, though. Somebody else could've hurt him wursa. He lucky to just have a broken shoulder. It's a good thang that boy of yours showed up. A few minutes more and we be planning for a funeral."

There was a silence for a moment, just the sound of forks on plates and cups on saucers and folks eating and drinking. I sat down beside Dah. He put a piece of bacon on my plate and spooned out some grits and eggs beside it. I felt like everyone was watching me as I ate. Dah had his hand on my shoulder. It felt like he was trying to reassure me that everything was all right.

From the kitchen window I saw a police car drive up on the side of the house, the sun beaming on its antenna, casting a silver streak of light through our window that whipped across the tablecloth. We could hear the dispatcher's voice on the radio asking for help in another part of town.

Two officers stepped out of the vehicle, grunting, adjusting their holsters. They looked in the backyard, then walked around to the front of our house and knocked on the door.

Mama walked to the front to open it.

Around the kitchen table it was dead quiet. Dah pinched the handle of the teacup and sipped his coffee. The sound of heavy footsteps preceded the officers as they came into the kitchen. Their white faces were red and serious under military crew cuts and Brylcreemed hair. One stood near the doorway, and the other approached the table.

He spoke for them both. "How're y'all doin' this moaning?" he asked.

Dah answered, "We all fine here."

Our two guests nodded their heads.

"What y'all need?" Dah asked.

"Oh, we don't need anythang, Brown. We just saw a few parked cars up on the sidewalk, mo'en usual, and thought we might check it out." Both officers looked around suspiciously. No one said anything. Dah kept his hand on my shoulder.

The policeman near the table rocked back and forth

on his heels, his hand on his holster. Taking a deep breath, he spoke: "Brown, seem like y'all okay here. That food is making me want some myself. And now that I see you got company, that 'splains the extry cars. 'Preciate your time."

Dah remained seated, and Mama thanked the police for coming.

They left.

No one spoke for a minute. Dah stood up and asked Buddy and Mr. Ray to follow him outside. Mama and my sisters cleared the kitchen table while I finished eating.

A Defiant King

One day I was sitting alone in the kitchen, losing respect for the plate of food Mama had sat in front of me to eat. Out of boredom I was mashing field peas between my fingers while holding my head up with my other hand, staring off into space.

Dah was away for work. My siblings seemed to have all eaten their lunch and disappeared.

I was startled by a rapping on the hardwood frame of the front screen door. I jumped up from the table and ran to answer it, thinking maybe Mama had locked herself outside.

It was a man whom I had never seen before.

"May I help you?" I asked, making sure to check that the door was latched.

"Yes, little sister. Is there an adult here?"

"Yes, sir, there is. What you want with her?" I asked, looking him over. The man wore a very white dress shirt, starched, with a little red bow tie, and his cuff links were gold and shaped like crescent moons. He had on a jet-black suit, which made him look important, although the jacket hung slightly off his shoulders.

"What yo' name?" I asked him.

"Daoud Khalil X," he replied.

Mr. X had a few newspapers in his left hand, and in his right hand he held a carton of eggs. He was clean-shaven. His shoes wore a spit shine bright enough to see my face in them.

"Okay, I'll go get her. You wait here," I said.

As I turned away from the door, Mama was coming inside the back door with the laundry she'd taken off the line, her eyes fixed on the silhouette of the man. She put the clothes basket on the floor and came quickly to the front door, wiping her hands on her apron.

Mama moved me away from the center of the doorway and kindly greeted the man. "How you? May I help you?"

"Yes, ma'am. My name is Daoud Khalil X, and I'm from the Nation of Islam. *As-salaam alaikum*, my sister," he said, speaking quickly. "Sister, I am here as part of the movement in Selma, and I am selling eggs today to raise money to fund our cause for the movement. Sister, could you help us out today? The eggs are fifty cents for the carton and the paper is free."

Mama instructed me, "Baby, go get my purse from the chair in my room, and don't go inside of it looking for anything."

When I returned, she took out a half-dollar, pushed the door open, and handed the money to the man through the door. The man handed back the carton of eggs.

"What did you say you doing here in town, sir?" Mama inquired. Before he could answer, she asked another question. "And where are you from?"

"Sister, we come here to be part of the movement for civil rights. We are here to help bring about the change that we all seek. Negroes want the same freedom as the white man. The freedom to move about as we please safely, and to vote, to eat, to sleep, to exist, and to live as we please. And we want equality. Yes, sister, my queen, we want to be shown the same respect as the white man. And, sister, I am from Chicago, Illinois."

With a slight step forward and his head cocked to one side, Mr. X asked my mother a question in the same breath as he answered. "Have you ever been to Chicago? Have you lived here all your life?"

Mama gripped the handle on the door and pulled it close to her. "Most of my life, yes. I was born in Choctaw County in York, Alabama. We are in Dallas County now," she said, pointing her finger down to the floor.

"Well," he said, "you must have seen a lot going on here, because I have seen things in Chicago and heard of things that, as a grown man, have caused me to weep."

"I know what you mean," said Mama sympathetically.

"Try to be as careful down here as possible. Watch your step and the way you look at these chere white people. They mad now, cause they feeling the heat on 'em and we ain't playing no more. This is it! We ready! And a lot of peoples are going to suffer, both white and Negro. And all I can say to you is be careful."

"It's been nice talking with you, my queen," he said, stepping away from the door. His bald head reflected the sun on its crown. "And I want to thank you for your support. I'm going to leave my nation's newspaper with you. Just promise me you will read it, and have your children read it as well. Don't forget to vote, and go out to the rallies. There's lots of meetings coming up," he said with a smile.

Mr. X placed a newspaper on the porch swing. Then he adjusted his shoulders to straighten his back, tucked the rest of his newspapers under his armpit, and stepped off the front porch, his raised head even higher than before. The sun rays glorified his every move, for which he seemed to mumble appreciation under his breath. He had found his swagger, moving off into the street with long black legs in black trousers connected to his shiny black shoes, and smoothly went to his next destination.

Mama and I had never seen anyone like Mr. X before,

nor had we ever heard those strange words, *as-salaam alaikum*. Mama said they were a form of greeting in his culture, but she didn't understand why he kept calling her a "queen." All our confusion was cleared up when we read the free newspaper he had given us.

After Mr. X left, Mama and I went back into the kitchen. As she took a Coke from the fridge, I quickly scraped my uneaten food into the trash and added my plate to the dishes in the sink, happy that Mama had been distracted from making me finish my unwanted meal. As I sighed and got ready to start washing up, Mama surveyed the state in which the dishes in the sink were arranged.

"I am going to have that talk with your brother and sisters tonight about how they has piled these plates and pots up here together. You children are always rushing. That's why me and yo' daddy always on y'all, 'cause y'all don't take your time. Move to the side and let me straighten out this mess before I start folding the clothes," she said, reaching over me and carefully removing everything from the sink. Then she filled it with clean soapy water and put the plates in. "Okay, now you can wash them without breaking anything. After the plates, do the glasses. You don't have much to do. It just looks like a lot, baby," she said, pinching my cheek before leaving the room with her cola to continue with her chores.

With another sigh, I sat down at the table for a while before I started, and thought of all my friends who were outside playing up and down the street. And where the heck were my brother and sisters? It wasn't my time to clean the kitchen. I needed answers, so I screamed, "Mama! Where is everybody, and why am I the only one home with you right now?"

Mama stopped folding clothes in her bedroom and came to the kitchen doorway. "You were napping when everyone left. Your brother went out in the country with Uncle Lott, and Chauncey is spending the night with your grandmother, so Noonchi took her over there. Lou is at choir and will be home in about an hour, and shortly afterward she's going to the pep rally at the high school," she said. "When we get the chores done, I am going to take a nap myself and then you and I can go over to the church."

Did she say "church"? I wasn't sure. Just looking at the mess in front of me and knowing that everyone was doing something more exciting made me angry. I called out to God, "Oh, Lord!" But I heard no answer. Then I called out to Mama again as she walked away, "Mama! Mama!" Mama didn't answer, either.

I knew Mama would be upset if I didn't finish the dishes, and I didn't intend to agitate her. But I had to call out to her once more because I was miserable. "Mama, I can't wash all of these dishes by myself. There's too many pots in here with stuff stuck on them."

Mama didn't like us calling across from one room to another. I knew she was just shaking her head and raising her eyes as she stood in her bedroom, folding laundry. Mama always looked toward the heavens when she was happy or vexed. I could just picture her pitching aside the laundry, falling back on the bed, trying to figure out why she had been given a mulish daughter like me.

When she didn't appear, I got up from the table and started on the dishes. A while later I had most of them done when I heard her footsteps coming toward the kitchen. I was scrubbing a black skillet, which was too heavy for my small hands. Mama reached over my shoulders and took hold of the cast-iron pan. "Not too hard, Hundey, you'll take off the seasoning," she said. "Why don't you dry your hands and go entertain yourself for a while until it's time to get ready? It's a special night and you are going with me."

"Mama, no. I want to go to the pep rally with Lou. She said I could. Not the church rally, Mama. Everybody will be at the school. Okay?"

"No, baby," answered Mama, "you are going with me.

Lou will be with Randy, and they are too old for you to hang around. This is more important. Now go play for a while and then put on some clean clothes and comb your hair, and we will take a cab to the church."

I interrupted, "But Mama, Lou won't mind, I promise."

I could tell Mama was tryin' hard to stay focused on the pan and not on my complaining. I knew she didn't want to start me crying over not being able to go out with my sister. I could see Mama was excited but also worried about the gathering, what with all the happenings going on in Selma lately.

Mama finished the dishes and went to her bedroom to get dressed for the evening.

I heard Lou stump into the hallway, rushing to the bathroom to freshen up. She washed and dressed quickly to get out of the house. I caught a glimpse of her as she stood near Mama's room, listening to her instructions. Lou wore her new cotton V-neck pullover and blue jeans. I felt the hot rise of jealousy swim through my head. I wanted to go with her. She passed by our bedroom and waved to me, I waved back and she smiled to make me happy. I started dressing quickly before Mama called me. After I got ready, I sprang into the room and announced my readiness to go to church with her. Mama was leaning back on the bed with eyes closed.

"Mama, um red' ta go!" I said with sass.

Mama sat up and walked over to the phone to call the cab. She cut her eyes at me. That was my first warning.

"This is Mrs. Brown calling. May I get a cab at Range Street going to Brown Chapel Church, please?" she said. "Okay, twenty minutes will be fine. We'll be outside, thank you . . . Oh! Who am I speaking with, please? . . . Okay, hey, Gina, how're you? . . . And what car number is coming? . . . Car sixty-five? . . . How is your mother? . . . That's good. Thank you! I'll talk to you soon. Bye-bye."

Mama made another phone call to let the neighbors know she and I were leaving home and to watch out for the other children when they returned and keep an eye on the house. Then she turned to me and instructed me, using the point of her finger, to go outside.

Cab 65 came on time. Lacey was driving that night, not his son. The trip to the church took longer than normal. An unusual number of people were in the streets and on sidewalks, all going to church. People were everywhere, walking, riding on bikes. Some cars had three passengers in the front seat and more in back, including small children, giggling and punching each other in the cramped spaces. The traffic was moving at a crawl.

Mama took a look at the gold Elgin watch on her wrist and mumbled something to herself as she leaned forward over the seat in front of her. "Let us out here, please. We are almost there anyway, and we can walk quicker than you can drive through this traffic."

Lacey pulled over, and Mama handed him two dollars. "Thank you," she said. "I hope you can get through safely."

"Sho' I will," said the driver. "Hit's all 'bout paychunce, all 'bout paychunce. And I'm hopin' he sho' up for us, aller us."

"What you saying, Lacey? You know better'n that. He's here, all right. I knowed since last week, quiet as it's kept. Ace Anderson let it slip. Now, Lacey, don't go back to the station and tell everybody, 'cause we don't want to spread it that much. Be cool! Hear me?"

Lacey reached in the glove compartment for change to give Mama, and she refused the coins.

"Missis Brown, I known you and yo' husban' ye'ahs. Dere's no way dis gon' git back to no un from me. You sho you don't want da change?" he asked with the two quarters between his fingers.

"I'm fine. Use it for the collection plate at your church. Brown won't miss it."

They both found laughter as we got out and Mama closed the car door.

Taking my hand, Mama looked at me and winked, saying, "He sho'nuf here. I can feel it."

I remained confused and angry about Mama's decisions. She had spoiled everything for me. The one time I'd been invited to watch a pep rally with my sister, Mama had to say no and drag me off to church to hear a visiting preacher preach. I was boiling mad.

Mama and I walked along the sidewalk with a host of others in front of us on their way to the church. As we entered on Clark Avenue, a residential area, I could see through the windows of some houses the flash of the evening news on black-and-white television screens, no doubt reporting on the war in Vietnam and the war going on around the country, where demonstrators were demanding equal rights for all.

Mama held on to my hand tightly as we neared the Carver Projects—and Brown Chapel Church. There were lots of shiny black cars parked along the streets, while white men in black suits and white shirts ran around with large cameras, taking pictures. I could hear the pop of flashbulbs and the click of their cameras everywhere, and wherever I looked there were children of all ages, some with parents and some in clusters with other boys and girls. Most of the children lived in the recently built housing projects and had become familiar with the everyday commotion of the civil rights activities going on around them.

Brown Chapel Church in Selma was the home base of the movement, and the Carver Homes temporarily sheltered many activists engaged in the struggle. Priests, ministers, nuns, movie stars, singers, Africans, observers, students, and Northern white protesters, people from all walks of life came forth to be part of the mass rallies, sleep-ins, boycotts, and marches in Selma.

Students took to dismissing themselves out of schools, like R. B. Hudson High, in order to be part of it. As students took to the streets, they were shouting and singing "We Shall Overcome." Preachers living in the area of the school would come out on the front porches and demand that any marches started must be peaceful ones. The preachers also demanded that we get out of the streets and stay on the sidewalks, and calm our voices down.

Old Negro women appeared behind screen doors of old, run-down homes and pointed dry old fingers, urging students to "Go on, y'all. Keep fightin' fo' yo' rights. God seed what they dun to us and he don't lak it. Y'all got the right. Jest don't let nobody tun you 'round."

And that's when the crowd would break out singing:

> *Ain't gon' let nobody turn me 'round,*
> *Turn me 'round,*
> *Turn me 'round,*

Ain't gon' let nobody turn me 'round.
I'm gonna keep on a-walking,
Keep on a-talking,
Marching up to freedom's land.

Ain't gon' let Jim Clark turn me 'round,
Turn me 'round,
Turn me 'round,
Ain't gon' let Jim Clark turn me 'round,
I'm gonna keep on a-walking,
Keep on a-talking,
Marching up to freedom's land.

Ain't gon' let Al Lingo turn me 'round,
Turn me 'round,
Turn me 'round,
Ain't gon' let Al Lingo turn me 'round,
I'm gonna keep on a-walking,
Keep on a-talking,
Marching up to freedom's land.

This was a call-and-response song, like so many civil rights songs. Mama later said those songs they sang in the movement stayed in her head every day for years.

When Mama and I finally reached the church, she urged me to quickly go up the steps, something I didn't want to do. So I hesitated, not wanting to obey. I stopped in my tracks and stood stubbornly on the steps. She took my hand and turned me around in front of her, and that's when she stared into my eyes without speaking. Her black eyes said it all. I reached for her gloved hand, glad to have the white cotton glove between us. I didn't want to feel the flesh of her hand in mine for fear of her reading my every thought. I was mad, so mad I could feel a hot tear roll out of my eye, down my face, and lock itself underneath my chin.

Mama stopped again, dead in her tracks, and stood in front of me, letting go of my hand this time. I lowered my head and eyes. I had been there before and knew Mama had had enough.

"Now you listen here, young lady. I have had enough of your snatching away, your sniffling, your whining, and your back talk. We are going into that church. I am not turning back, and you are not going anywhere with your sister. Now you take that handkerchief out of your pocket, wipe your eyes, blow your nose, and straighten your face out before we go through that door. And you got less than one minute. Do you hear me?"

I nodded in agreement and followed her orders this time.

"Hundey, if you show your behind up in this church tonight, I will spank you right here, right where you stand,

and then tell your daddy on you when he comes off the road. Do you hear me?" she asked.

"Yes, ma'am," I replied, "I hear you." I relaxed my hand in hers and let the cool, crisp air blow through my head-scarf as we went up the stairs. I kept my other hand in my dress pocket, and I simply forgot about the ball game. Strangely enough, I felt that my crying and the lecture she had given me had done me some good. I felt better and soon began to take in the evening.

Once inside the church, Mama and I found seats as fast as we could because it was filling up quickly. We sat three rows in front of the pulpit on the right side, where two of Mama's friends, ushers, came over to talk to us. Mama asked them to stand in front of us while she prayed. She said King was late and she felt the need to pray.

I didn't understand what she meant at the time about King being late because most older people called God *King* and it simply didn't mean anything to me at the time when she said it. One of the ushers sat behind me as the others stood. Mama was sitting, rocking, with her head bowed, and started singing her prayer, but there was so much commotion only I could hear it:

Gotta call on you today, Lord.
Something's happening here,

Got to call on you today to tell you about something going on here.

The Devil's got loose in Alabama and he's waging war on the people.

The Devil's loose in Alabama.

He showed up in the seat of the house of power,

Showed up on the police force,

Showed up in the White House,

He showed up on the roads in Alabama.

I want to tell you what we need you to do, Lord.

I want you to call Gabriel,

Telling him to perch the angels on the back roads,

Perch them in the trees,

Seat them in all the churches,

You know what to do, Lord.

Help us, protect us, and stand by Martin Luther King

'cause he gone take us in the right direction.

He gone take us to Montgomery.

Be near him, Father. Aaahmen!

My mama finished praying and the ushers moved on. I was excited to see all the children, men, and women— many we had never seen before. They all had come to see *Kang,* as they would call him in a hard Southern accent. I looked around while Mama sat quiet. There was so much movement and commotion as the ushers walked the aisles and helped to sit people. Cameras with big bright lights and thick, snakelike cords were set up in the back. Ladies had begun to fan themselves from the heat of the lights, and someone had started singing a song, and after that someone else started a song, one that stayed in Mama's head.

The songs weren't always started from the beginning. Some were sung from the middle . . . *"Just like a tree that's planted by the water . . ."* As this beautiful singing went on, and somebody was singing, and somebody was singing, and somebody was singing, people sat and talked, laughed, and greeted each other with handshakes and hellos.

Someone came onstage and announced that everybody should try to find a seat. The singing and joyful chatter stopped.

I was standing near my seat when suddenly I saw a man in a gray suit behind us pointing in my direction, toward the dais. He screamed, "There he is! There Kang!"

I turned around to see as people rose up from their seats and started calling his name, clapping, jumping, holding their heads, hugging each other, stomping, dancing, praising God.

"Kang, Kang, Kang! Dere he is."

I didn't feel Mama's arms around me, pressing me to

sit down. She had tears streaming down her face when I finally heard her saying, "Sit down!"

I sat down but couldn't take my eyes off this well-dressed, short, stocky man. He was there! Right there in front of me. His face was brown and smooth, and the collar on his white shirt was whiter than the ones we soaked in lye soap for Dah.

"Look, baby! Hundey! That's Kang!" shouted Mama. "There he is! Whoo! Whoo-wee! Yes, suhh! Thank you, Jesus! Kang! Kang! Kang!"

Clapping, more jumping. "Lord! Oh, Jesus, it's going to be all right now! KAAANG!" These were the chants and feelings and cries of the people in the church that evening. All the people, young, colored, white. And the children, so many children. As the old people say, we "tore the church up" with all our jumping and shouting.

Dr. Martin Luther King Jr. walked slowly across the dais, took his position on the pulpit, and, looking out on the crowd, raised two well-cleansed palms. The people sat down and became quiet. Only the rustling of fabric on the church benches and the shuffling of shoes could be heard.

Then Dr. King began to speak, and the voice and the words were not on the TV or radio. I was in front of him, and my mother was there. I heard him say: "We have the right to vote. Just give us the ballot." So surreal was his voice, which mesmerized me, and the charisma of the time, with the unfolding of events and this giant of a man stepping forward to bring justice at any cost to the people, hypnotized me.

I grew limp and trembled under the sound of his voice. His voice was like a dream, a dream that I dreamt each day while listening to the radio. Mama grabbed hold of me and rocked me back and forth as she listened to his words. My head lay on her chest and I could hear her heart beating fast as her tears fell from her eyes and into my hair.

Dr. King did not speak long. Soon he was ushered out the church as the loud enthusiasm continued. By then we were all standing up to sing "We Shall Overcome," with arms locked together and swaying. We sang from the bottom of our hearts with smiles on our faces, smiles that drank the flow of tears that ran from our eyes, with no hands to wipe them away because everyone's arms were locked together as we sang.

After Dr. King left, we heard from other speakers, but I don't remember anything else. Eventually we were dismissed. The people were so jubilant, leaving the church for home. One of Dah's friends offered us a ride that we accepted. Mama sat up front with the driver and his wife. I sat in the back with two other people. Everyone talked about how well King spoke and how good he looked.

How he had outsmarted Jim Clark, the Dallas County sheriff who wanted to prevent King from speaking.

I listened and held my arms around myself for fear of taking flight. I held myself against the heavy steel door of the car because it was the strongest thing that could keep me from flying away. I heard Mama tell the grown folks that I wasn't shy. I was overcome. I would be all right when I got home, Mama said. The lady in the back seat kept looking at me, and she touched my hand and blessed me. But I never turned to look at her.

Later that night, I asked Mama why Dr. King had stayed such a short time with us.

She replied that King had defied an injunction temporarily halting civil rights activities, and that was why he'd spoken quickly at Brown Chapel that evening. And from there he would be going to speak to the youth in another church. King knew the people were ready, and he did not want them to lose the momentum.

After seeing Dr. King that night, my thoughts and mind were now set on freedom. Selma was changing. And I was changing. The door had opened for me.

A Baptism

On Sundays the doors to Selma churches were open wide and people could be seen making their way to service. Organ music filled the neighborhoods and guided the parishioners on their way, bringing with them all their concerns of the weeks past through the doors of the church and placing them in prayer before the altar. New worries, old problems, sickness, gratitude, and uncertainty found their way to the church in shined shoes and pressed hair as fancy clothes turned heads and Avon sachet-powder scents blew through the air, giving the church a fresh start on the morning.

The preacher welcomed everyone to "come just as you are" while the choir hummed the words to "Come to Jesus," rocking side to side as the people made their way to their seats. And now, Selmians were hearing a different kind of preaching on Sunday mornings because the time for change had come, and Selma was beginning to embark on a movement of nonviolence with a campaign for equal rights. Selmians had decided to begin pressing the government to desegregate the schools and to allow Negros the rights to register and vote.

I started watching more news reporting on television to enhance my awareness of the movement. We owned a Sylvania TV and a telephone. We had a wringer washer machine, too. A new room had been added onto our house and painted. I do not recall a time when we did not have a truck or a car. We also had newspaper subscription and delivery, and a subscription to Johnson Publishing Company magazines. Our family had Life of Georgia Insurance on everyone in our home. Dah was a member of the Lodge of Freemasons and Mama was an Eastern Star usher. Our faith was Baptist, and we all attended John the Baptist Church in Orrville when Dah could drive us, and Ebenezer Baptist Church in Selma when we needed to walk to a church closer to home. My three older siblings were baptized in the river behind John the Baptist Church in Orrville. The day before they were baptized, Lou, Ben, and Noonchi were bathed from head to foot and kept in a room and prayed over nearly all night. They could not talk or look out the window or fidget too much. No television. They had water and some bread to eat, and Grandmama was one of the praying people in the room with them. The day they were going to be baptized at John the Baptist, I was not invited to go to the church, so Grandmama told me what would happen. She said, "Reverend Blevins will meet everyone at the church at ten a.m. and they will all have prayer and blessings. From there a procession of people will walk to the lake all dressed in white and meet the pastor, who will be standing in the lake, and he will call each person in the line by name. Then he will receive them in the water and take them under, because you have to go under the water to be saved and have the Holy Ghost Spirit put in you, which will save them, give them a new life."

After the baptism, the saved ones were prayed over again, and then fed a proper meal, and for one week they had to be righteous, and after that "sin no more." I was glad that it was all going to be over soon, and although I would miss watching television with my siblings, especially the Johnny Carson show each night, at least I would have someone to talk to again.

When I heard Grandmama say that Reverend Blevins in Orrville had asked my sisters and brother not to sin anymore, that stayed on my mind. I decided to call Ebenezer Baptist in Selma and ask them if I could get myself baptized. The deaconess who answered the phone said that I could, and that it would not be held back from me if I wanted to do it and that she would not mention it to my mother, but I should. She said that she would talk it over with Reverend Reese, and if he said that it was okay, which he probably would because this was the Lord talking through me to be baptized as soon as possible, Reverend Reese would perform the ceremony. I asked her if I had to be prayed over all night and stay in a locked room. She said that would not be necessary. Reverend Reese was a preacher of modern days. She said it was the right thing to do because no one wanted to die and go to hell. To me, being in Selma was a form of hell. So I walked the few blocks to meet the woman at Ebenezer one morning during the week and signed my certificate to be baptized. I had to stay one step ahead of Satan before I became a teenager and before I marched for freedom and civil rights or engaged in a sit-in.

I was baptized in Selma by Reverend Frederick Douglas Reese. Saved! I had taken the responsibility of getting baptized because I felt that my mother was taking her time in saving me by waiting on Reverend Blevins in Orrville to wade me in the water behind John the Baptist Church. After baptism I received my certificate but didn't show it to my mother until I thought she was ready to see it or when I felt she was fixin' to have me ducked under the water with all those snakes and people constantly praying in my ear. Weeks passed, and one day I showed her my certificate. She was happy. "Well, now we have ourselves an official member of the church in Selma. Save some money so you can pay your tithes," she said.

One Christmas

Should we decorate the tree tomorrow?" Mama asked from the doorway of the dining room on Christmas Eve. None of us answered. She repeated herself a bit louder. "How 'bout we put the lights on the tree in the morning, 'cause it's too late now and your daddy's waiting on his plate?"

No response. As an early Christmas present, Dah had come home from his job yesterday with a brand-new television set, a Sylvania, and everyone was watching an episode of *Gunsmoke*, my favorite Western.

Mama raised her voice. "Did anybody hear what I just said?"

Dah was sitting at the table, watching the show as well. None of us children had noticed his presence in the room. I knew Mama was staring at me as usual. I turned around and rose from the floor quickly.

"Yes, ma'am, it's okay by me. We can do that just like what you said. I will set the 'larm clock. Okay?" I volunteered, although none of us ever slept late on Christmas.

Our new TV was shaped like a box, with four blond-colored legs, each one capped with brass covers at the bottom. The television was our fourth most important household feature. The telephone was the new number one most important device we owned. Then there was the radio, and after that was the box of stationery and a book of stamps that were kept in a drawer near the phone table because our family wrote letters even if the recipients were only five miles away.

Dah pushed the dining room chair away from the table and crossed his right leg over his left knee. "No, you don't have to make them wait. I'm not tired, Kate," he said gently to Mama. "Just let them children have fun with the program they watching. Um gonna sit here and watch it with them while I eat my supper."

Mama returned to the kitchen with his dinner and came back in a few minutes.

Dah looked up from the TV and surveyed his new plate of food that Mama had placed in front of him. "Thank you, hon. Maine, when the next commercial come on, will you go git the Christmas lights out the trunk of my car, please? Your grandmama sent them over here for y'all to enjoy. She said she has no use for them anymore as far as decorating her place and that by now Santa should have hired a Negro man and his wife to help distribute some of those gifts around here. Yo' grandmama said that Santa was one of the oldest living humans on earth and important as he is, he should be able to hire anyone he chooses. But since he hadn't hired anyone but them elves, and none of them were from Africa, she was done with old Mr. Saint Nick. She'd rather see the joy in y'all faces than to have the lights and thangs waste away in the attic over there."

Just then a commercial advertising Tide detergent came on. Dah spoke up again. "Maine, get the newspaper, too. It's in my chair on the front porch. I'd like you to read while I finish eating. I'll help y'all light up the tree as soon as I'm done. Go 'head," he said to Maine with a wave of his hand. "And turn that noise down a li'l."

Noonchi turned down the volume and Maine ran off to get the things Dah had asked for. He returned with the lights and a newspaper and sat next to him at the table, spreading the paper flat and reading aloud the articles one by one on the front page.

Suddenly the Western stopped, and the words SPECIAL BULLETIN appeared on the screen. We called to Mama to come quick, even though Dah was sitting right there. She came quickly, our fingers pointed to the screen. The only thing she spoke was "Shhh." No one moved. Maine didn't close the newspaper for fear of the noise it would make. He laid it on the divan carefully and quietly waited for the news bulletin.

The news clip showed Negroes and whites protesting segregation at a restaurant chain in Atlanta, Georgia. The protest had been going on for days. There was a sit-in at one of the lunch counters, and there was a white police officer watching. We learned that one of the demonstrators at the counter was John Lewis of the Student Nonviolent Coordinating Committee, but we couldn't hear his words. We saw outside scenes, too, and bystanders gathering. We learned that many of the protesters had been arrested and jailed, including Mr. Lewis.

Mama and Dah watched in silence, and we knew to be quiet and serious, too.

The news told us that the protesters had been charged with trespassing but they refused to pay any fines and made it known they'd spend their Christmas in jail rather than pay. And more demonstrators had been arrested today on Christmas Eve, including the wife of comedian Dick Gregory, who they said was pregnant. The news report said the protesters had found a way to handle their legal problems.

I couldn't understand the whole story, but Mama and Dah were listening close, and we children knew they were hearing something important. The news stated that the protesters had some ownership shares in the company that owned the famous Toddle House restaurants where they'd been demonstrating, and their lawyers said this gave them the right to be served.

The bulletin ended, but we never got to watch the ending of *Gunsmoke* because Mama asked us to turn off the TV set.

We all sat silently on the floor, waiting for our parents to instruct us on the next thing to do for the evening. I heard Dah slide his plate aside, and his fork fell to the floor. He left it there.

I wanted to hear what my parents had to say about the arrests, but no one spoke. They just stared away into the room, both seemingly worried. Quiet.

The breaking news had struck my parents, and it wasn't the first time news like this had intruded on our lives.

But this time my parents made sure it would not cause us to rearrange our lives, which right now meant they made sure we would not miss out on decorating our new Christmas tree.

In the past our Christmas trees were small and had sat on the table near the picture window in a corner, and the gifts were stacked around the legs of the table. Mama wanted a larger tree this year so she could put one of her beautiful Gee's Bend quilts around the bottom of the tree stand and place our gifts on the quilt. She also wanted us to take part in dressing the tree together as a family, because so many families were losing their members to the struggle going on out in the streets in Selma, across the state of Alabama, all across the country. She would say, "You never know when you leave out the do' the next time you'll see each other again."

The new tree was huge, and we had purchased all sorts of fancy decorations from Boston Bargain Store and the Kress Store to make it look beautiful. I named the tree, calling it Little Thumbs because at the end of each of the branches were three fingers that spread out like thumbs.

Little Thumbs would stand proud in front of our picture window, the first really big Christmas tree we had in our home ever. I had heard one of our neighbors say that all good Christians should have a big tree. And now we did. It was a thick, luxurious one with a perfect green color and undertones of ashy blue underneath its branches. We were all so excited to have a Christmas tree sitting in the middle of our living room window, a tree that dazzled everyone who walked past our home with the spirit of celebrating the advent of Christmas and the hope of peace.

Dah had gone into the woods of Dallas County with his dogs and Maine to get the best fir tree they could find, at Mama's insistence. He managed to get one that stood over seven feet tall, with big, luscious branches. When the tree came through the front door, I tried hugging it in hopes it would hug me back. That didn't happen. I almost toppled over its branches had it not been for Dah's big boots in the way. Just the presence of Little Thumbs changed our whole house. Even without decorations, it was still quite beautiful.

It took a while to get the lights on the prickly needles. The heavy Christmas lights had to be placed carefully on the limbs where they sat behind the branches and appeared as if the light was born of the tree. Decorating took time, even with all of us working together hanging paper snowflakes, shiny tinsel, plastic cupcakes, painted pine cones, and pretty round glass balls that cracked easily if dropped, revealing a silver lining. We were careful in holding them, and we let the tallest person hang them in the highest spaces and the smaller hands reached the tightest places.

Our Christmas tree was finally finished, standing graciously in the room like an elegant Japanese empress shrouded in a beautiful kimono.

"Well, look at that," said Dah. "Now I don't feel so bad about cutting it down. Y'all come on. Let's go see it from the outside."

Everybody rushed outside to the sidewalk to admire its beauty from the picture window.

"I think it needs to be moved over to the right side

a bit," Mama said, "'cause if you look at it from where I'm standing, it's not in the middle . . . You see where the coffee table is?"

One of us on the sidewalk answered, "Uh-huh."

"Well," said Mama, "go on in there and move it a tad over. Watch out here and I'll tell you when to stop. Don't push it too hard, 'cause you'll spill the water inside the tree stand and wet the floor."

One of us ran into the house and followed Mama's instructions carefully, then returned to our little sidewalk crowd.

"We forgot the angel!" shouted Mama.

"I'll get it," Dah said. He dashed inside the house for the angel and placed her glassy pink wings gently over the top branch of the tree, directly in the center, and positioned one of the bulbs to shine underneath her gown, and she lit up. Then he ran back outside to us.

"Oh, darn it, we forgot one more thing—the paper dolls we made in school," Noonchi called out.

"Where are they?" Mama asked.

I said I had last seen them on the dining table near the newspapers.

"Well, I have a thought," Mama said. She suggested we put them on the tree as an homage to the protesters who had just been arrested outside the restaurant with Mr. Lewis. They were freedom fighters. And they could have a special Christmas with us although they were physically jailed.

"As soon as we go inside, you all start hanging the paper cutouts around the middle of the tree in the front, and draw the curtains over the window. We don't want any trouble with no one thinking us all uppity with our big ol' tree at this time. We still have to be careful how we act even though it's Christ's birthday."

"Yeah, your mama's right," said Dah. "Ol' Jim Clark and that ol' Bull Connor n'em don't care if it's Christmas or Easter, they are always looking for something they can accuse us of."

Jim Clark, Dallas County's sheriff, was always looking for trouble or trying to make trouble out of no trouble. Both he and his crony Bull Connor, Birmingham's Commissioner of Public Safety, had spies everywhere, reporting to them.

"And believe it or not, there's sneaks running around here in town who are evil enough to spread rumors and lies for a piece of bread or fifty cents. Desperation is a jealous thief," Dah said.

All our shoulders were erect as we stood looking at our tree in awe and pride. Christmas was here and all of us were together.

That evening, our handwritten letters to Santa were attached to the tree so that he could read them when he got to our house. I had written Santa asking for a doll baby, which was all I wanted. I dreamt of him and his elves reading my letter and picking the best doll for me from his sleigh and placing it under the tree. Once all the gifts for our house and our neighbors were under the tree, Santa would dash off to another home and fulfill more wishes. My sisters and brother had told me that usually Santa starts delivering gifts around the end of Thanksgiving, and that's why decorations of turkeys and colorful corn tied on doors were taken down, and wreaths of holly and pictures of Santa would appear.

My favorite picture of him was a magazine ad with a red-and-white Coca-Cola sign with a puffy-cheeked Santa underneath, with a curly white beard and white hair, holding a bottle of Coca-Cola and flashing a cheery smile. I can remember staring at this picture on the back cover of a magazine during the holidays and wishing that one day maybe I could meet Santa. But I also wanted to meet the Negro Santa my grandmama wanted Santa to hire to help with Christmas. Grandmama said that she would make a special fruitcake for the Negro Santa to eat at our table. She said that the Negro Santa did not eat cookies and drink milk. She said he probably ate homemade fruitcake and *drunk* black coffee just like Dah did. Perhaps the Negro Santa would know exactly what kind of doll I'd like, since he was just like me.

Christmas morning came and we all ran into the living room. A bleary-eyed Dah turned the tree lights on, while Mama was sitting at the table in her housecoat, waiting for her coffee to finish perking. She looked tired, but she smiled seeing us entering the room.

"Y'all couldn't wait, could you?" she said.

"Well, go ahead, chillren," Dah said. "See what's there for you."

Gifts that hadn't been there when we went to bed spilled out from under the tree. Packages were being checked for names and gift boxes held up and shaken. Paper torn. Wrappings balled up and thrown to the side.

I found two gifts with my name on them, but no doll could fit in them, so I passed them up for later. I walked around the tree near the window and there was a shiny red girl's bike with a tag on it bearing my name. I was happy and confused. I had so wanted the doll. So why did Santa give me this bike?

I carefully guided the Santa-red bike away from the window and into the middle of the floor. I liked it very much.

"Go 'head, get on it. It's yours," said Dah, standing in the dining room with a white coffee cup in his hand.

I'd never had my own bike before. This one stood up high with two white sidewall tires and training wheels off the sides. From the handlebars hung red-and-white tassels, and there was even a rack behind the seat on the back. I could pull someone on it, give them a ride around the block. How nice!

"Don't you want to see what else you got for Christmas?" asked Noonchi. "You have a box and one other gift. Come see." I didn't respond. The bike was so pretty to look at. I wanted to go outside right at that moment and find someone to share my joy with, but Mama said it was too early and too cold. She wanted us to eat breakfast before going outside. She had already made the oatmeal and scrambled the eggs. The toast was thick slices of homemade bread that had been given to us by one of the church ladies.

After breakfast lots of children would be outside with new gifts to show off. From the living room window, I could see the children beginning to gather on each other's porches or riding their bikes on the sidewalk. I pulled my new bike into the mudroom and grabbed my coat before Mama could stop me. Maine helped me get the bike out the back door and out onto the sidewalk. I got up on the seat and started pedaling. The pedals were stiff but I managed to push as hard as I could to get going. Suddenly I was riding a big-kid bike. I waved to Mama in the window, watching me take my new ride up and down the sidewalks. I rolled around the corner and back again and again, stopping to see my friends, who admired my bike as I examined their new toys.

After riding for so long, my legs were tired and it was getting colder. Mama was still in the window when I stopped the bike at our gate to run inside for my gloves and a hat. I came out again to find my friend Bruce, who had stopped to look at my new bike. He asked me for a ride. I didn't want him to steer and pedal the bike. I wanted to pull him around the corner on the back of the bike. Bruce got on the rack. He was heavy. I kept trying to move the bike but I couldn't, so I told Bruce to get off, and once I started to move, then he could jump on. Bruce got off. I started pedaling, and once I got going he took off running and jumped on with such force his weight broke the back rack from the frame and we both fell off onto the cold ground. The bike was ruined, with pieces bent this way and that.

Bruce was apologetic and ran away sadly.

My friends started coming over to see what had happened, but I was not able to face them. I left my bike where it fell and limped inside, where Mama was waiting for me. "You shouldn't have put him on the bike. He is too big."

I burst out crying, and she wrapped me in a hug. Mama sent Maine out to get my bike. Dah was in the bathroom taking a bath, so Mama took me to the kitchen sink to wash a scrape on my hand.

Then she told me to go sit quietly in the living room until it was time to get ready to go to church and Christmas dinner out in Orrville.

I could not believe it was still Christmas morning and my new red bike from Santa was already gone. I was torn up inside.

There were still two gifts under the tree bearing my name. I went over and opened one of the boxes. It was a small metal tea set. I put it to the side and started to cry. What use was it to me? I thought.

My sister Noonchi must've heard me crying. She came into the room where I was sitting on the floor. I didn't want to look up. My eyes were full of tears and I hurt.

"Maine's out back working on your bike. I bet he can fix it, Hundey," she said, sitting down next to me. "Here now. Why don't you open this last present? Maybe it's something special."

I raised my head higher and she handed me the gift. Slowly I tore off the wrapping paper. There, on my tearstained lap, staring out the plastic window of a small box, was a small brown-faced doll, just big enough to have tea with me from my new tea set that I had opened and pushed to the side.

My heart was filled with joy. The little doll could fit in

my sweater pockets and go everywhere with me. I threw my arms around my sister's neck and thanked her for the gift.

"Don't thank me, thank Santa," she said. "Or maybe a Negro Santa, I don't know."

I was not sad anymore. I had exactly what I wanted for Christmas, and she was my doll.

"Let's go have a cup of cocoa and a slice of fruit-cake while we think of a name for your doll," Noonchi suggested.

I named the doll Cookie, I don't remember why, maybe because it was my cousin's name. But I will never forget the Christmas tea party the three of us had.

Mama was in her room with Dah, resting before it was time to go to Grandmama's house.

"While she naps, let's not make any noise or leave any dirty dishes for her. Okay?" Noonchi said.

Cookie and I thought that was a very good idea.

Camden

In 2016, Lou and Ben relayed their stories to me regarding an incident that happened in early 1965, when the teachers and students of Richard Byron Hudson High School were planning to protest for the right to vote.

One day in February 1965, Reverend Frederick Douglas Reese and Principal Joseph Yelder decided to close the Richard Byron Hudson High School, where my sister Lou attended eighth-grade classes, and Maine was a sophomore. The school closed for the day because Reverend Reese was planning to have the schoolteachers march in support of voter registration for Selma's Negro citizens. Older students, too, were planning to join the march. Reverend Reese was a math and science teacher at the school and the head of the Dallas County Voters League, an organization created to register citizens to vote.

For teachers, it was a frightening yet necessary decision, frightening because they could lose their jobs, yet important enough to the movement as a show of solidarity and strength for Negro children and their future.

After class dismissal, Lou went home and found no one there. After waiting a while to see if Noonchi or Maine were coming home, she decided to go to her friend Lily's home to spend the rest of the day with her. She did not want to be alone.

When she got to Broad Street, which was near the high school, it was closed to traffic and there were several buses parked on both sides of the street. An outpouring of students and teachers on the sidewalk was being overseen by police officers, and Sheriff Clark was in the center of the mayhem.

Trying to figure out the reason for the buses, Lou spotted her boyfriend, Randy, and they raced toward each other.

"You should go home right now. This is dangerous," he said.

"Why?" Lou asked him. "What's happening?"

"Listen to me—" he started to say, but Lou had seen our brother, Maine, coming out from behind one of the buses, and she ran toward him, leaving her boyfriend behind. Soon Randy was lost in the crowd.

Ben took hold of her arm and also encouraged her to go home. He said the teachers and students were getting ready to march.

But by then it was too late.

The police began to encircle the protesters, and suddenly my brother and sister were caught inside the circle with the teachers and many of the senior high students from the school. Chaos was setting in.

Now Maine was yelling at Lou: "I told you it was dangerous! Why didn't you go home right after dismissal?"

"Ben, I did go home, but there was no one there, so I decided to visit Lily. I don't know where anyone is right now!"

As Lou and Ben spoke, one policeman ran to another right in front of Lou and yelled, "Put all these here nigger kids on the bus, right now. We got lots of nigger children here. Put 'em all on the bus. Get 'em now! Get all of 'em and take 'em downtown!"

Ben held on to Lou's arm as the other officer yelled, "There ain't no room downtown! Go find out what the sheriff says!" Then he hollered at all of the kids standing around the buses: "You people need to go home now!"

The crowd did not disperse.

A few minutes later, the sheriff's orders were clear: Maine and Lou and dozens of others were all packed into the many buses by officers with billy clubs. On their bus, children were screaming and crying until two policemen on the bus threatened them, and then everyone got quiet.

Soon the buses were rolling, south across the Alabama River on the Edmund Pettus Bridge. *Away* from Selma.

Maine recognized the route the bus was taking. He whispered to Lou, "I think we're going to Camden. There's a jail there."

They arrived at the prison in Camden, Alabama, near seven p.m. It was out in the middle of the countryside, surrounded by trees hanging with eerie Spanish moss and dense underbrush.

As they stepped off the bus, an announcement was made by one of the officers through a bullhorn. He said, "Sheriff Clark told us to tell y'all that this is where y'all will stay because you didn't go home when we ast you to."

As Maine had thought, "this" turned out to be the jail in Camden, which was populated with hardened criminals. Most members of Ben's and Lou's group were youths, and many had begun to cry again, some uncontrollably. The teachers and senior high schoolers became their temporary guardians, consoling them with hugs and kind, soft words.

After being marched into the yard, an exercise area of the prison, the Selma protesters were all put into large fence-enclosed bullpens. At first women and girls were kept apart from the men and boys, but then they were allowed to mingle.

According to the prison guards, Sheriff Clark had sent word that the detainees would remain there in Camden until further notice. Lou found these words all the more frightening, because he'd already had them arrested and hauled off to a place far from home. This seemed completely illegal and yet it had happened anyway. Lou's thought was, *If he can get away with this, what else will he do under the law—his law?*

During all this confusion and sadness, she found one of her friends, who was always making jokes, even at this time, so it was good to have her there. Then she saw another friend, Maine's girlfriend, Evelyn. It was getting late and they were all hungry.

Lou suggested they try to find Maine, who she knew was still holding the money given to him by Mama that morning to pay bills after school. Lou knew Mama wouldn't be upset if they used some of the money to buy food from the vending machines located at one corner of the yard.

They found Ben and managed to get through the crowd and to the vending machines, which dispensed Lance's cookies, candy bars, and cigarettes. After a meager snack, they were still hungry.

Toward evening, Ben remembered the jailers entering

the yard and directing the crowd to a dining hall. The smell of food took away some of the pain the detainees were all feeling. Their portions of beans, cornbread, fried chicken, and collards were not heaping platefuls, but the meal was good and hot. Maine and Lou were surprised to learn that the inmates had cooked the meal especially for them.

In the cafeteria, the protesters ate alongside the inmates. The prisoners were polite to the protesters, treating them with respect, although they couldn't touch them or say much. The guards kept close watch while everyone ate.

After dinner, guards led them to the Selma protesters' cells, where they were crowded like animals alongside the convicted criminals. Maine watched in dismay as his sister and girlfriend were led away to a separate cell from him.

In the crowded cells, when women had to use the toilet, the men gave them privacy, turning their backs. Someone would hold up a blanket as a screen. And if the women and young people like Lou were overcome with grief, hardened criminals were heard offering words of encouragement, helping them through this first night in jail.

The following morning, as he was eating breakfast in his crowded cell, Maine saw the head cook, an old Negro man, walking slowly past each cell as he surveyed the prisoners. He did not wear a smile on his face. He glanced in

Maine's direction and nodded toward him, raising his left shoulder a bit. Had he added a bebop, Maine thought his movements would have resembled a dance.

Maine understood that the cook had come out from the kitchen to show solidarity with the protesters in appreciation for their sacrifice. As he passed by, the detainees said, "Thank you, sir" and "God bless you," and he nodded as he saw the waves of little hands through the cell bars. His wrinkled and worried face said it all: *Come what may, if this is the last thing I do in my life, then this is my glory right here.*

Later that morning, Maine was out in the exercise yard but did not see Lou or Evelyn. One inmate sitting on a bench close to him in the pen spoke out to a crying woman. "Ain't no sense in crying, little susta. Ain't no one gon' bother you in hare." The inmate extended a thick black hand with yellowed talon-like nails to give her a piece of toilet paper to dry her face.

To a crying older detainee, the inmate said, "Muh dear, you mo' stronger than me 'cause sometime I cry for days and I'm stuck here. Now we all here together. En we gon' fight together. No mind that sheriff!" His voice softened. "He already dead. Stay in here wit' us, in high spirits."

Then he gave Maine a cracked smile. He pointed to three inmates, possibly friends of his, sitting on the ground in a corner of the pen. "You see Jebadiah, Pole Cat, and Li'l

Man over there? They don't b'long here. They was set up out there. Now, lot of us b'long here, to tell da troof! But them dere," he said, pointing fingers at the three men, "they don't b'long here. When they first came here, they cried all night, and Pole Cat fought all the time. Now ever'body all right together. It ain't all good, but it seem like y'all goin' through mo'n we." He shook his head. "Struggles for the Negro man don't seem right." He handed the crying woman another piece of paper. "Here, now stop crying. You stronger now."

The woman looked up at him and smiled, and he smiled back.

Days passed and more people were coming on buses. An estimated total of 1,500 protesters were soon to be locked up. The jails were full already, and more demonstrations were happening outside. It was hot and stinking in the jail in Camden, Alabama.

Maine and Lou and the other protesters were there for seven days, and during their time spent in jail, no one harmed them. Not one woman was touched or stared down. Not one man was challenged to fight by prisoners. The only violent and abusive activity they had experienced was from the Dallas County Sheriff's Department, from men who were deputized by Jim Clark and who had been sworn in as good citizens of Selma to protect the Selma community, who were now illegally and blatantly disregarding the law and changing the rules, holding people behind bars without cause. The actual prisoners behind bars, the convicted criminals, behaved more humanely to them than did the sheriff and his deputies. These lawmen were free to kidnap teachers and their students and take them deep into the backwoods of Alabama. They were free to hold them hostage for days and nights behind bars, as though they deserved punishment for standing up for justice. These police terrorists did all this evil in the name of the law, and nothing was ever done about it.

Word got around that Sheriff Clark was enraged after finding out that protesters were being treated well by the other prisoners and even by the prison staff. He didn't want Maine and Lou and all the other "agitators" eating up the county's food supply and being treated with Southern hospitality. He called the warden and made his orders clear: "Give 'em beans and rice just like any other con in jail! Them all the same! I got a right mind to come out there and beat that there cook's ass myself," he said before slamming down the phone.

The inmates who were "trustees" based on good behavior worked in the prison library and had menial jobs in the administrative offices. They were the ones who brought the news back to the other inmates about the sheriff's call to the warden.

The prisoners, hearing this report, found Jim Clark's rant amusing and made fun of his anger for days.

It was over as suddenly as it began. After a week passed, news arrived that Dr. Martin Luther King Jr. had gotten all of them out of jail.

"There's buses coming to take y'all back to Selma!" a guard announced loudly. "They on the way, so y'all can git red' to go."

Maine watched some people cry with joy and others praise God for the glory of being set free. Women pulled up dresses and pulled down slips, finger-combed their hair or borrowed hairpins to clamp down rough, wiry locks. Men unbuttoned and rebuttoned sweaty, wrinkled shirts, tucking them into soiled pants, tightening loose belts, smoothing back kinky hair.

As they lined up to board the buses, many shook their heads in disbelief at the experience they had lived through. Then the gates were opened and the detainees walked out to board their caravan back to Selma.

In line to board the bus, Maine was happy to see Evelyn and Lou standing together ahead of him. He yelled to them, "Please call Mama when you get home, and stay together."

They nodded in agreement.

Maine passed some coins to them through other people standing in line, so that they could make phone calls once they got back home.

Lou and Evelyn boarded the next bus, and the bus that followed would take Maine out of Camden and into Selma. Seeing them leave and knowing he would be next rejuvenated him and his thoughts became clearer. A light breeze temporarily erased the bitter reek of his own filthy clothing and that of those around him. All that he could smell was the woods, the soil, and the fresh air.

As passengers began filing onto the next bus, Maine joined the other men in stepping aside to allow the women and younger students to board first. Then he climbed aboard and claimed his seat near a window, just as the smell of the last seven days rose again off his clothes. The driver didn't want any windows open behind him except for his own, so the ventilation was poor. Where Maine sat, a wisp of air blew through a small crack in the window, and my brother kept his face as near the opening as he could.

He was so tired and frustrated, he wanted to cry. Thoughts he'd held back for days now tumbled through his head. *How could this have happened? How could people be so cruel to us? What did we do? All this time we've been locked ille-gally in jail, sleeping on floors or cots, waiting for news of our fate, while the people of Selma, the white people, were home with their loved ones, going about their lives. Most of them do not care what is happening to us, or they do not know what is happening to us, or they do not want to know what is happening to us.*

Maine and the other traumatized passengers were dead silent the whole ride. Maine hugged his arms around himself and wept, glad that Dah was not there to see him cry. So glad that his sister and Evelyn were not there to see him break down.

When his crying ceased and his chest no longer heaved, he tried to sleep. He watched the cars fly by the bus in the night. Most of them were driven by white own-ers, because Negroes were told by preachers and activists not to travel late on the roads in Alabama, because some roads were illegal for Negroes to use, and traveling on dirt back roads was dangerous at times. Dah often took the back roads as a shortcut to Montgomery or Orrville or Sardis, Alabama, when he had to "run a package" to someone. When he went out of town, Dah carried a green book that helped him find places that served the needs of Negroes. Things like food or gas. Dah also had a red can that he used to store extra gasoline in case he ran out, a dangerous situation to be caught in.

That old night seemed endless and held a strange

feeling for Maine. The whole way, he couldn't shake the feeling that something terrible was going to happen to their bus or one of the buses in front of or behind theirs. He tried to close his eyes and forget the feelings but they were very strong, like the warm odor he smelled coming from his own body and the man's body next to him. He positioned his head closer to the window and caught a nostril full of fresh air, which momentarily lifted his spirits as he breathed it in slowly.

Maine repositioned himself, stretched his back. Just then he noticed a car that seemed to be driving along with the speed of their bus. It slowed down once or twice, and he caught sight of a white woman at the wheel with a passenger in the front seat. The odd thing about the passenger was that he was a young Negro man. Maine knew this was dangerous. He couldn't believe it. A white woman and a Black person sitting together in the front seat was unacceptable in Alabama. He looked around to see if others on the bus were witnessing what he was seeing, but they all seemed to be sleeping.

Before the woman in the car accelerated on the gas and disappeared into the night, Maine was able to get a glimpse of her face, and strangely, he sensed that he would see her face again. Weeks later he saw a news flash on television about the death of Mrs. Viola Liuzzo, a white woman who had just been ambushed and killed on a lonely Alabama highway while transporting a young Black man from a civil rights activity. She closely resembled the woman Maine had seen that night, driving alongside his bus.

When his bus finally got to Selma, it parked at the end of a long line of buses outside the courthouse. As they disembarked, police told the detainees to make their way into the courthouse for processing. As they filed into an already overflowing courtroom, the judge approached the bench, clearly disturbed, and stated furiously that no one would be processed because the stench and the number of people did not permit it.

"Get those people out of this courtroom and this courthouse immediately! And get those janitors in here to clean up this place!"

One of the court clerks told the judge that the janitors had gone home.

The judge lashed back, saying, "I don't give a hoot if ever'body in town is sleeping or having supper. Get those janitors in here and I mean it. This is a crying shame to bring these people up in heah this way in my courthouse."

He slammed the gavel down hard and flew out of the courtroom, a black canopy of robe floating behind him.

And that was the end of it. There was a hush and then someone said, "Jesus! Great God a' mighty!"

Everyone left the building smiling, because their stench had prevented them from being charged with a crime they had not committed. Right don't wrong nobody!

Outside in the fresh air, my brother found Evelyn and Lou. The two of them were trying to get a ride home, so Maine flagged down a passing car that had room for two passengers. It turned out that he knew the driver, and that the man and his son were willing to drop Lou near our house and take Evelyn all the way into East Selma, which was farther away.

Maine wanted to walk home to clear his mind. It was only a mile or two and wouldn't take long.

A few minutes later, the driver dropped Lou off. She said goodbye to her friend and walked along Range Street into our driveway.

Dah was sitting on the front porch where he always sat, the light from the Rutger family's service station down the street revealing his silhouette. She was surprised to see him because he was supposed to be in Kentucky, working. He asked Lou where her brother was. She told him that she had left Ben downtown near the courthouse about twenty-five minutes earlier, and that Ben wanted to walk home alone.

He asked her how she was doing and she said, "Dah, we were all together in jail—me, Evelyn, Miss White's daughter, and Ben. And, Dah, we went through a lot, but we are all okay."

Dah listened, then went inside a moment and came back out carrying a paper bag. He stepped off the front porch, sat down in his car, checked the glove compartment, lit a cigarette, and drove off into the dark night without speaking another word.

Lou watched him go, then walked into the house, calling out to Mama and Noonchi and me.

Meanwhile, to get away from the crowd, Ben had walked over to Water Avenue and then turned up Washington Street, heading home.

Before too long, he saw a car that looked like ours. It was Dah. He was in Selma.

Maine hollered until Dah spotted him. He pulled his car over in front of Washington Street Supermarket and parked front-way in. He jumped out and walked straight into the street to reach his son, ignoring the traffic.

"Come on, Maine. Come on, git in the car," he said.

My brother rushed across the street, dodging a few slow-moving cars, as Dah opened the car door for him.

"Maine, are you all right?" he asked after he pulled out and motored slowly back up Washington Street.

"Dah, we been down in Camden, in the jail."

Dah nodded like he knew this already but didn't say anything. Eventually, he pulled the car over to the side of the street, and cut the motor, and asked Maine to tell him everything they had gone through.

After Maine finished telling him what happened, they sat there in the car, just sittin'. Maybe Maine was waiting on permission to cry in front of his father, I don't know. But Dah kept his eyes straight ahead like a bird dog, staring at the dark street and black trees in the night. Finally, he relaxed his right shoulder on the car door and turned toward his son, breaking his silence.

"Maine, you gon' stay over here at yo' grandmama's tonight. I stop by here before I came lookin' for you to let her know that I was going downtown to find you and brang you here." He did not take his eyes off his son. "Your sister is up in the house with your mama and Noonchi and Hundey taking care of them, and I just figure you be better off here. I'll 'splain thangs to Kate when I git back to the house."

Maine hadn't realized they were sitting in front of Grandmama's till Dah mentioned it.

Dah continued, "We going through the back door where the bathtub is, and she has already got thangs ready for you. So you come on out the car now and go on inside and git right in the tub. Everythang you need is in there already. Take off all your clothes and put them in a paper bag. I'll throw them in the burn bin later. I brought over a change of clothes for you, and there's a toothbrush and comb in there, too. Wash your hair good."

Dah opened up the back door and they went in.

Maine turned to face him. "Dah, may I ask you a question, sir?"

"Yeah, Maine, go ahead," he said.

"Dah, how come you home?" Maine asked.

Dah now stood with his back to his son as Maine undressed. "We got word up in the railroad camp that thangs were heating up down here. It was Don Garrett's wife who called up there like she do ever week to check on him and give him any news. She told him about the protest and that you and Lou had been picked up off the streets and arrested."

Maine got into the tub as Dah continued. "It didn't make sense to me as to what Don's wife had said, and I knew your mama would be upset, so I went to the boss and told him that I had to go see 'bout my family in Selma. Don was on his way home, and I came on into Selma with him. He said that his wife had heard that Sheriff Clark was so scared of us Negroes that he had locked up his own children in the courthouse jail with him, for their own safety. That made me madder than before, and I wondered what kind of man we were dealing with. I knew long ago that Jim Clark was racist, but to what degree would he go to hurt people? When we got to Selma, I told Don not to take me home. I told him I was going to see King."

Maine froze in the steaming-hot bathwater. "Dah, did you get to see him, sir?"

"Well, Maine, when I approached Brown Chapel, the people there told me that he was at Tabernacle Baptist in a meeting, so I walked on over there. It was about eight men there that I met, big ones, standing in front of the basement door. All them folks that us'lly be around him, taking pictures and writing, were not there. All them big cars were gone, too. Jus' a few cars parked in the back, back there. When I told them I was there to see Dr. King, they were very polite and asked me if they could be of help. I told them that my children were locked up and I wanted to know why and that I had come all the way out of Kentucky from my job on the railroad to get my children out.

"One of the men told me to wait there and he would be right back. The others ast me if they could search me and I told them to go 'head, but that I had a pistol on my leg. They searched me and took my gun. Then the other man came back and told me that King would see me. Son, I had no doubt in my mind that if he was there, I was going to see him. I didn't try to figure it out, I knew it.

"The men came back to git me, and we went downstairs, one in back of me and the first one in front of me. Dr. King was standing between two men, and a Negro woman was standing to his right. One of the men who had met me outside spoke into Dr. King's ear, and King whispered something back to him and stepped forward to speak to me. He told me that eventually everyone in jail would be released within days. They were working on the release at that moment. He told me, 'Not to worry. They can take it. The children are able to take what's happening to them. It might be hard on the adults, but the children, believe it or not, are enjoying it, and we are making progress. Mr. Brown, we are going over that bridge and we need your support. Your children are protected. They might be scared, but they will come through.' We shook hands and I thanked him for seeing me.

"One of the men escorted me out the door. The men standing outside told me that they didn't believe what they had just seen, the fact that Dr. King would see someone right away without an appointment. They gave me my pistol, which was unloaded now, and I went back to the car, where Don was waiting.

"Now, Maine, don't mention this to your mama. What I told you is 'tween us. There's a war going on in Selma as well as across the water, in the 'Nam. You and me been riding 'round Selma since you were four years old. I wrestled you from Kate when you were six, and at seven, you could drive a tractor. You know me better sometimes than yo' mama does. What's happening here in Selma, Maine, is going to change the world. Men are fighting each other for freedom from mental and physcul slav'ry. We are not free yet. Lot of us gon' get hurt or die. Women and chillren's fighting, too. This is big.

"Listen to me careful. From now on, if I'm not home, you stay close by. I mean that. Yo' mama won't handle a gun, and neither will yo' sister Noonchi. You go find Willie Mae or Lou and give one of them a shotgun if you need to. They know what to do wit it. I showed 'em. Maine, don't tell them two anythang thatta scare 'em unless you jest honest-to-God have to. And don't carry any of my thangs with you anywhere, showing off and attracting attention. I mean that, too. You hear me?"

Maine nodded in agreement. After hearing all this from Dah and agreeing to obey his wishes, he got dressed in the clothes Dah had brought him and they went into the living room to see Grandmama.

Maine bent over and shook her hand, kissed her, and broke down in her lap, crying. Dah helped him up and took his boy to the bedroom nearby. He sat on the edge of the bed, next to his son, holding his hand until he fell asleep. As he drifted off, Maine could hear Grandmama praying in the living room. He woke up about four in the morning and went out to find Grandmama still awake in her rocking chair, with the Bible open on her lap. Dah had gone home to be with Mama and us girls.

Frankie

We were awakened late one night by Mama walking into our room and shaking us to get up quick. She yelled, "Y'all, we got a call, and we got to go to Beloit." Beloit meant the same place as Orrville, and most of the time we said Orrville more than Beloit. It didn't matter, though, because we knew where we were going no matter which name was called.

My aunt Susta, Dah's sister, lived out thataway. Mama said we didn't have to change our clothing from pajamas and slippers to regular clothes and shoes, so we knew something was going on. We grabbed a blanket, and some of us were picked up and carried to the car or ushered carefully out of the house to the station wagon parked in the driveway. We all piled in, asking no questions, just finding a spot to sit in or stretch out on or in someone's lap. As we were driving, I heard Mama say to Dah, "She sounds so tore up. She kept saying, 'Git Daddy out here. Y'all come quick as you can, we don't seem to have much time left!'"

Ainty Susta's nickname for Dah was "Daddy," and because he was her children's uncle, they called him "Uncle Daddy." We took the back roads, as we often did to avoid the sheriff and save time. Dah drove fast. I could tell how fast he was going by the gravel spitting off the car tires, hitting the back bumper.

When we got to the house in Orrville, Dah was the first one to strike out of the car and head for the front porch. It seemed as if he was flying, climbing the steps to the porch and front door.

Ainty Susta was at the door, pointing. "He in there, go right on in. Pastor's in there, too," she said, reaching for Mama's arm.

We trailed in from the car in our pajamas and slippers, and some way, somehow made it to the steps ourselves. Someone put me into a high quilt-clad bed with my cousin Cookie. There were a few people in the house other than my family, and they were all quiet and somber.

A yellow-striped cat came over to the bed where I was to meow at me. I flinched.

"You scared of cats, Hundey?" asked Cookie. "She just a baby, she can't hurt you. Here, let me show you. Rub her back, she soft. Come on, take just one of yo' fangers and rub her back."

"I don't want ta rub her back or see her face. I don't

like cats; just get it out of my face. I don't like the way it looks," I said, cringing.

"Okay, you don't have to play with her if you don't want to."

The cat was put on the floor, and I felt at ease. But soon that cat found its way back onto the high bed. I screamed, and almost had an accident.

Mama came rushing out of the other room to see what was happening. She ordered my cousin to "take Hundey to the toilet," which was outside in an outhouse, and "leave the cat out there for the night until we go, please."

Mama returned to the other room, leaving the door slightly open by mistake. After being scared to death nearly, I was fully awake now, and quite curious to find out what was going on inside the next room where the adults were gathered.

Cookie helped me down from the high bed and gave me my house slippers. Sliding on her shoes, she instructed me to stay behind her.

"It's pitch-black out there. We gon' use the moonlight. Hear me?"

I nodded in the dark. Cookie seized the cat, and as we passed by the next room, the door was cracked enough for me to see inside. I could see Frankie, my cousin, lying in Ainty and Uncle's bed covered up to his neck.

His head was resting on a white pillow, turned toward his left shoulder, his eyes closed and his lips swollen. He was not moving and neither was the Bible on the table by his bed, which was supposed to protect him. A white doily lay stiff and starched under the Bible. A bedside lamp, whose light was low, was casting off shadows.

Something was wrong, and it showed on the faces of the people gathered in the room. I became bewildered, and I did not feel good about this night. I noticed that someone sitting in a chair behind the slightly ajar door wore shoes that I didn't like. They seemed to have a meaning behind them that troubled me deeply, yet I couldn't understand what the meaning was at that moment.

My cousin urged me to move faster. I stepped outside into the darkness with her, moving fast to the old outhouse that was their toilet. Cookie put the cat down and it scampered off into the bushes. All I saw were treetops illuminated by a bright sliver of moon and one billion stars. Alabama nighttime.

I noticed that Cookie carried torn pieces of newspaper in one of her hands and a complete sheet of newspaper in the other. She cracked the door to the shed open and placed the newspaper over the wooden seat. I sat down, trying to push out the pee-pee as fast as I could. I did not wait to wipe myself because something was buzzing in the hole, and the moon was watching me through the cracks in the shed. I pulled up my panties and my pajamas quickly and left the newspaper on the seat. My eyes having adjusted to the dark, I ran back to the house behind Cookie, entering the kitchen just as Mama was coming out of Ainty and Uncle's room to check on us.

Mama hurried us back to bed. She left the door to our room slightly open, and I heard her and Maine talking out in the hallway. They were speaking in whispered voices, words I couldn't hear. The tense feeling in the house carried me into a fitful sleep.

Before long I was wakened again as Dah and Mama and Maine helped the rest of us all get back into the car. On my way out I noticed that the door to the other bedroom was closed tight. We had spent only a few hours visiting with Ainty Susta. We arrived home in Selma exhausted and crawled into our beds, tired and unsettled.

A few days went by and we were told that Frankie had passed away. At the age of sixteen, at home, with his mama Ainty Susta and his siblings at his side. He died from meningitis, we were told. After hearing this news, all we could do was cry. Then stop and cry some more.

Frankie was someone who played with us—his younger cousins and his sister. On the first Sunday in every month we were likely to be at his house after church.

Sometime before we ate dinner we would explore the country, walking on the red roads or hiding out in the barn, looking at the hens or at other times picking figs off the fig trees. The pomegranates were left alone. "Do not pick them in the nice clothes you wearing," Mama cautioned. "They not ready yet." We flocked together, saying little and having fun.

Those days were gone now, and the reality was a death in our family. The loss brought all of us to sadness and tears. My aunt Susta, ripped of her son, questioned the Lord's actions over and over as to why he had taken her child. As fist-pounding grief tore the bitter tears from her eyes, she praised the Lord and thanked him for the blessings to have had a son like Frankie.

I can remember us as children wanting to stay inside the house listening to grown folk talking, but whenever they noticed us, we were shooed outside. We didn't play much now but mostly sat around on the front porch, three of us crowded onto the swing, the rest sitting on the steps, not talking much but staring at the surrounding woods and fields, listening to the buzz of insects, pointing out a high-flying hawk or a red-bellied squirrel messing about at the tree line.

If we made too much noise, Mama or another adult would open the door to quiet us down and keep us outside so that we wouldn't come trotting back inside and make Ainty Susta's cake fall in the oven. She was never without an apron, and her hair was tied up with an old rag to keep the sweat off her brow. Inside her apron was a handkerchief pinned to the inside pocket with which she could wipe her tears from time to time. A small silver tin rested in the other pocket. Ainty dipped snuff. She'd take a pinch of it from the tin and put it into her bottom lip. When it had lost its purpose, she would turn away and spit it out into the trash. Always polite and warm, she had a dignified grace that kept her grounded in life.

The service for Frankie's funeral was going to be held in nearby Hazen, at Aimwell Baptist Church. His family was expecting Frankie's entire school class to attend. Relatives from different states were preparing to come.

The pastor called to say the church would be full. That was when Mama declared that the youngest children would not be going. This meant me and Chauncey. She said that Grandmama and them, Susta and her children, would be mourning and she didn't want us looking at them or getting afraid of what was going on during the funeral. Other relations were going to drop off their youngsters, too. "Y'all being there would put too much pressure on your ainty's spirit, which is already broken by now. With you all there she would hold back, and that's not good for her health. She's got to let go her emotions. I'm going to get my brother Robert in Choctaw County to come up here to help with y'all. We taking the older ones who want to go to the service with us."

At that moment I started to cry, and Mama wiped my face with her bare hands.

Since I was kept away from the funeral, I never had a chance to say a proper goodbye to Frankie. His death remained such a puzzle. If he had meningitis, how long did they know he was sick without telling us? Had this disease crept up on him? How did he get it? Would we get it? I remember asking Grandmama about that. She said none of us were sick from Frankie's ailment, because "God had watched over us."

We were obedient children, and therefore we believed what our guardians told us. Meningitis, we had been told. So we left the matter alone for the time being. No one talked about it after the funeral. Frankie's name seemed to vanish.

My brother and sisters and I, we grew out of Selma, one by one, setting out for other places to live, some to towns and cities where relatives could be found, helping us to start our own lives, others to places altogether new. We started our own families but never stopped calling long-distance, writing letters, and making holiday trips back home.

When I left home at nineteen, I wrote letters and

called and visited everyone often. There was always news to share, gossip to hear.

I never forgot Frankie, never stopped wondering about his death. I knew there was more to the story than what I'd been told. Many years later, I started to get answers.

One day I called to speak with my uncle Early in Detroit. The only living relative on my father's side, Uncle Early was of a sound mind at the age of eighty-nine and loved to hear from his family and to talk about "back in the day."

As our conversation advanced, he asked me about my children, and I in return asked him about his niece Cookie, still living down in Orrville. Cookie, whose given name is Cora, my cousin Frankie's sister. And after asking about Cookie, I found myself asking my uncle about Frankie's death.

Earl's tone of voice changed as he asked me in turn, "What do you know about it?"

I simply answered, "We were told he died from meningitis."

"I've heard that also," Earl said. "But the talk, if you want to call it so, is that Frankie was with a white girl, and he had been arrested because of it."

I had learned to wait on the truth, knowing that it would come one day, and I remained steadfast in patience until truth stopped by my door one day and laid its burden down. When my uncle Early told me about Frankie,

I exchanged the heavy baggage that I had been carrying for decades and picked up the lighter grip offered, and breathed a sigh of relief. I listened as Uncle unloaded his account of the matter, revealing what he knew.

"I heard of the girl's ex-boyfriend, a white boy, witnessing them together and telling them that he would tell his father. I heard that the father of the jilted white boy passed the information to the girl's father, and he in turn passed it to the sheriff. One day Frankie was arrested, just coming home from school or something, and you can guess the rest. For heaven's sake!"

I could feel the truth of Uncle Early's words warming my whole countenance like sunlight. Based on what he said, I began piecing together what may have happened to Frankie, and none of it was good.

Having hesitated for years as to whether or not I should speak with family members on Frankie's side about his death and according to what my uncle had told me, I knew now was the time to inquire before someone else died, taking the truth with them.

When I called my sister Lou to tell her what Uncle Early had reported, Lou told me something that had been kept from me by all of them in the family who'd gone to the funeral without me. That one afternoon, not long before the night when Dah had taken us all to Ainty Susta's in Orrville, Lou and Mama had received a call to come to the hospital fast and that something had happened to Frankie. When Lou and Mama arrived at the hospital, Lou said Ainty Susta was out of her mind, crying, "My boy, oh my boy. God help me with my boy." There were tubes connected to machines and tubes in Frankie everywhere. The doctors at Good Samaritan Hospital were doing all they could, they told Ainty Susta.

Lou also told me about a dream she had had as a young girl, the night we were told that Frankie had died. Lou had witnessed Frankie's funeral in a dream, and a few days later the real funeral that she attended with my parents was exactly as it was in the dream. All his friends and family members were there, except us youngest ones. She told me that it was not Frankie she saw in the casket in her dream. "It was you, Hundey, that I saw in the casket in my dream."

All my life I have had visions, and what Uncle Early and Lou told me did not surprise me. Frankie's death had haunted me for decades, and if I told you that I have seen his fight for his life unfold, you would ask me how, and I cannot explain it to you.

The conversations with my uncle Early and my sister Lou had unlocked my fear of opening old wounds, and I was determined to call Cookie in Orrville and raise the subject. I sat on the flat arm of the sofa, holding my cell phone to my ear, waiting for the phone to ring in Cookie's house. The connection was slow, which may have had something to do with how deep in the woods of Alabama she lived. I was anxious to hear Cookie's robust voice sounding like Ainty Susta's. The connection happened, and her hello was nothing like her mother's until she started to speak more. I could tell that she was surprised by the call, and I took my time speaking so that she would understand my reasons for calling. Although I felt guilty of presenting her with this task by opening up her life once again to review her brother's passing, I simply could not hold back.

Some say that people who live alone in their own homes have a tendency to speak loudly. "Hello, Cora!" I said, loud and quick.

"Willie Mae?"

"Uh-huh."

"How's everything?" she asked.

"Good, good. Is this an okay time to call you? There are a few things I'd like to ask you."

She replied, "This is fine. I'm here. I can talk. What's on your mind?"

The guilt passed, and I presented my reasons for calling. "I would like to speak with you about my cousin's death, your brother, Frankie."

"Okay," she said.

"I would like to know what happened to him when he passed away."

"What is it that you want to know?"

"What I want to know is how he died, because I have heard things, and I would like to know if those things hold any truth that you know about. I have spoken to Uncle Early and he has expressed some things, and one of the things was that Frankie had become involved with a white girl, which may have been the cause of something happening to him by the hands of others, if you know what I mean. What did you know about this?"

"Willie Mae, what I know is this. Frankie did get arrested, and I did hear something about a white woman or a girl. Frankie was just sixteen years old at the time, and he was in jail overnight. We got a call at some point and Daddy Lott answered the phone and told Mama that Frankie was in jail in Selma. Lott called Mr. Hansen, who owned the land Mama and Daddy sharecropped, and Mr. Hansen went to the jail and brought Frankie home."

Cookie said that the fact was they were young and they couldn't ask too many questions. They accepted Frankie being home and not in jail, and they all sat down to watch television that next morning. At some time during the program they were watching, Frankie suddenly began to have a seizure, and Ainty Susta called out for someone to get a spoon to put in his mouth so that he would not swallow his tongue. Frankie had never had a seizure before, and Cookie said they were scared when Frankie was taken off to the hospital.

Cookie recalled that after a few days in the hospital, the doctors dismissed Frankie to come home, "because there was nothing more they could do for him," they said, and that had led to us converging on Orrville late that one night. I asked her if Frankie had been ill before he came home from jail and had a seizure, and she replied, "No, he never had any problems, and Mama took us to the doctor often." I asked her if he looked uncomfortable or sad, and she said that he was quiet, but sometimes he was quiet. I asked her if Frankie had worked in the fields recently and she said no. It was October and all the crops were in. I asked her what did his death certificate read, and she said that his death certificate said that he died of meningitis. Then, to my surprise, she said, "But Willie Mae, it was known in Alabama that doctors put down things on a death certificate or even a birth certificate that may not be true. I have accepted his death. It is in God's hands."

I asked her how did her mother take his death, and she said that it was not easy. Sometimes she would catch her mama crying, and Cookie would try to ask her things about Frankie's death, things that Cookie did not elaborate on with me, but she said her mother did not want to talk about it.

When a person has meningitis, especially in those days, the household is checked for meningitis, quarantined. Neither Cookie's family, nor my family, nor any other person in that house died or was sickened by meningitis. I told Cookie that Uncle Early had told me that he was sure that something happened to Frankie in the jail that caused his death within a few days. I questioned Cookie about the night that we had gathered at Ainty Susta's in Orrville, and she said that she did not remember too much about that night because there had been so many people in and out of the house, and, because we all often gathered there, that it was just something that we were supposed to do, or someplace we should be at a time like that, so it was not something that she remembered very well. But she did say that she remembered the funeral service and Frankie's classroom students being there and the church being overcrowded that day and how sad it was.

Cookie also said something that I had known for years. She said we could never ask any questions and never get a straight answer on anything, especially if it was something relating to a problem. They would always wave you away and tell you that they would take care of it. Growing up in Selma I was aware of the secrets and the private ways of its people. Not many people were quick to tell their business or discuss their lives with others. In Selma, if you wanted to know something about someone or something, you could ask, but the response would usually be vague. At times one could be told to "Go ask your daddy," or "You shouldn't be asking me that question," or "You are a child and you should stay in a child's place and let the grown folk take care of this." And, "Who told you to ask me that question?"

I was always offended by these answers, and I tried to be clever in the most appropriate way to get an answer. "Mama, how come I can't ask that question? Is it wrong for me to do that?" A question such as that received a vague answer, possibly silence. So my strategy was to listen, to listen carefully and to see. To see all that I could see the moment I entered the room or on the street or in a car or the church. I learned to read expressions and listen to thoughts, which is something you must truly master. But the most valuable strategy was patience. Patience and good health will bring the answers. Patience is conviction. Just wait. And watch. Watch their movements, look at their eyes, and see if they turn up their nose as if they are smelling something. Did they raise an eyebrow? Did they flick you away with a hand wave? Because most of the time this is what happened, and when it happened I knew that I was onto something. I learned to wait even if it took years, convinced of getting an answer to my questions.

In the 1960s when Frankie died, the lives of Negroes were still vulnerable to death without justice. You could come up missing, or you could catch something the doctors couldn't cure. And then you were buried and silenced. I believe what I have always believed: that something happened to Frankie. Now, whether it was in a field before he was taken to jail or at the jailhouse before Mr. Hansen brought him home, someone had something to do with Frankie's death.

The memory of that night haunts me, the night we were taken to Orrville, where I saw Frankie in bed with his head resting strangely to one side.

Frankie, Frankie Finnegan! I felt your pain. I felt your pain because I have the ability to sense these things. (You know what I mean.) The night I saw you in that room, I had to leave the scene and go inside myself so that I would not hurt, because the pain was too much for me to stand. You are my first cousin, blood-close. Now that I have written about you, and the stories are on their own, you are not in my thoughts as much as before. Because you have called out to me, and asked me not to forget you, I will call your name whenever I read these stories aloud! Frankie! Frankie Finnegan!

AFTERWORD

My narrations open up the wounds and itch the scars that I and Selma's people carry. My voice will not be quiet, nor will I quiet the voices of those who gave me the talk. I wrote my stories of Selma, for it is also their story—their hearts, and prayers, and voices. My voice is their voice and I will never forget my Selma!

And here is where hope for the future lies. Hope is in the telling. Hope is in our voices and in our stories that we share as a tool of freedom.

Hope is in our stories that free us and allow us to reach into the hearts of others and give them the freedom to speak as well.